Beethoven's
Fifth and Seventh Symphonies

A CLOSER LOOK

MAGNUM OPUS

Edited by Robert Levine

Magnum Opus is a series for anyone seeking a greater familiarity with the cornerstones of Western Classical Music—operatic, choral, and symphonic. An erudite collection of passionate, down-to-earth, and authoritative books on the works and their creators, Magnum Opus will build into an indispensable resource for anyone's musical library.

Forthcoming:

Bach's St. Matthew Passion, by Victor Lederer

Handel's Messiah, by Ben Finane

Brahms's Symphonies, by David Hurwitz

Beethoven's
Fifth and Seventh
Symphonies

A CLOSER LOOK

David Hurwitz

continuum

NEW YORK • LONDON

2008

The Continuum International Publishing Group Inc
80 Maiden Lane, New York, NY 10038

The Continuum International Publishing Group Ltd
The Tower Building, 11 York Road, London SE1 7NX
www.continuumbooks.com

Library of Congress Cataloging-in-Publication Data

Hurwitz, David, 1961–
  Beethoven's Fifth and Seventh symphonies : a closer look / David
Hurwitz.
      p. cm.—(Magnum opus)
  Includes discography.
  ISBN-13: 978-0-8264-2944-5 (pbk. : alk. paper)
  ISBN-10: 0-8264-2944-0 (pbk. : alk. paper) 1. Beethoven, Ludwig van,
1770–1827. Symphonies, no. 5, op. 67, C minor. 2. Beethoven, Ludwig
van, 1770–1827. Symphonies, no. 7, op. 92, A major. 3. Symphonies—
Analysis, appreciation. I. Title.
  ML410.B42H87 2008
  784.2'184092—dc22

                                              2008028620

Printed in the United States of America

To Lena and Hannah Myers,
the next generation of musicians in the family!

$\mathcal{C}$ontents

Introduction

 *A* Closer Look

WHEN ASKED ABOUT HIS HESITATION in writing a symphony, Brahms famously replied, "You have no idea how it makes me feel to hear the footsteps of a giant such as Beethoven marching behind me." Without pushing the comparison too far, suffice it to say that similar thoughts must occur to any writer starting a new book on Beethoven as well. Both the man and his works enjoy a vast and distinguished body of literature, so any addition necessarily needs to spend a little time defining its aims and placing itself in the context of a singularly imposing out-pouring of commentary and scholarship. Beethoven's symphonies, in particular, have been the object of everything from the most abstruse kind of technical analysis to the fluffiest popular discus-sions. Most writings, including this one, stand somewhere in the middle, and it's a very broad "middle."

So let me begin by first explaining what this book is *not*. It is not an investigation of the Fifth and Seventh Symphonies along strictly technical lines. Most often, this approach is synonymous with some sort of detailed harmonic analysis, a convenient method because harmony and tonality are entirely describable in verbal terms according to an accepted academic nomenclature. However interesting this may be to the specialist, it offers very little useful information to the listener because it says next to nothing about orchestration, dynamics, tempo, timbre, melody—in short, all of the things that normal people hear in the music in actual performance. From the listener's point of view, this is akin to trying to get a picture of a magnificent building by reading a minute description only of the type of concrete that went into it.

Even musical examples are nothing more than symbols, a shorthand code standing in for the genuine article. This book never requires that you be able to read music. If you can, and feel so inclined, then by all means go ahead and purchase the relevant scores and consult them as you deem helpful and appropriate. Otherwise, the ability to read music or follow a score is no more necessary to understanding a great piece of music than knowing the chef's recipe in order to enjoy a fine meal at a famous restaurant. Neither the chef nor the composer expects or requires it. Just as your palate lets you identify individual flavors, so your ears will tell you all that you need to know as you listen, and words are just as valid as musical notes in helping to isolate the various ingredients that constitute the complete dish.

On the other hand, a great deal of popular literature dwells extensively on historical, biographical, or psychological detail at the expense of engaging the music itself. This sort of description focuses on the backstory as an indicator of what the music supposedly "means," as opposed to what it does and how it sounds while doing it. Although this approach certainly has its place, it should complement discussion of the music and not replace it. There is, in classical music writing, a very strong, and to my mind very sad, tendency to try to sweeten the pill for the average reader, to assume that individual musical works are not intrinsically interesting and explicable in simple language. From this combination of elitism and insecurity arises a great deal of what has come to be called "music appreciation," the notion that the classical music repertoire can't simply be enjoyed as can any other type of entertainment.

Let me get right to the point and state categorically that I firmly believe not only that Beethoven's symphonies are eminently enjoyable and approachable without any need for special training or reference to related historical or biographical issues, but that this *is* what makes them "classics" in the first place. What this book is, then, is a description of two wonderful symphonies, fortified with enough additional information so as to place them in a useful musical context for active listening. Practically speaking, the biggest obstacle to understanding any large piece of classical music, particularly in today's media-saturated world, is resistance to the notion that it's reasonable to spend large chunks of time (and be satisfyingly entertained) primarily using your ears above all other senses. Once past this initial leap of faith, Beethoven's music does the rest.

My purpose, then, is to suggest various entry points and pathways that will take you straight to heart of Beethoven's Fifth and Seventh Symphonies as quickly as possible, trusting the music to work its magic from that point on. After an initial discussion of the historical and biographical context surrounding the creation of each work, I will consider both symphonies in detail, with reference not just to their noteworthy and outstanding features, but also to the earlier works which may have inspired them, and some of the later pieces that adopted them as models. While undeniably and inimitably unique in countless ways, Beethoven's symphonies are also part of the larger continuum that constitutes the Western musical tradition, and they can and should be considered as valuable guides to many other equally enjoyable musical treasures that you can discover at your leisure.

This, then, is a book about listening, first and foremost. The discussions of the two symphonies are too long and detailed to be used to follow the course of the music while reading and listening simultaneously, in real time. They stand independently; but the information that they contain is almost entirely directed at what the music sounds like, what it does, and how it expresses the feelings that you, the listener, experience whenever you hear it. This means that you can read the rest of this book in any order, including the general essay on Beethoven's symphonies immediately following this introduction, and then listen to the complete works, or approach them on a movement-by-movement basis. Whatever works best for you is fine.

I will also mention in passing quite a few recordings of each symphony, and in particular point out which versions (of the hundreds available) will most clearly allow you to hear special moments or points of characteristic significance. Previous guides that I have written have either included actual CDs or ignored the subject of recordings entirely given the chaos that reigns in the classical music recording industry. Today, however, the availability of inexpensive (even free) digital downloads, not to mention "on demand" custom CD pressings and international online ordering, means that an unprecedented number of performances are readily available, and seem likely to remain so. It will be a particular pleasure for me, then, to take this opportunity to introduce you to many of the best and most noteworthy names in Beethoven symphony performance and recording.

At the end of the day what matters most to me, and I hope to you as well, is not coming up with something "new" or "original," but offering something useful and, above all, *accurate*. Music is a highly subjective field, whether in performance, criticism, or scholarship, but behind it all lies the enduring reality of what Beethoven wrote over two hundred years ago, and it is this essence, the physical presence of sound moving through time, that has thrilled countless millions of listeners right through to the present day. The totality of "the Beethoven symphony experience" can never be captured precisely in words because its impact on each listener varies constantly with each new encounter. But the fact that a magnificent landscape may look quite different as the seasons change does not mean that its basic features aren't recognizable or describable.

Beethoven's Fifth and Seventh Symphonies, while not exactly landscapes, have more than enough verbally identifiable features to give you a strong feeling for their emotional terrain. From this beginning, the pleasure of experiencing their inexhaustible variety on repetition will then be yours to discover. Speaking personally, after several decades of serious listening, they have never grown stale or ceased to amaze, and I have no doubt whatsoever that, having gotten to know them well, you will agree. It's a huge pleasure and privilege for me to assist you in reaching that point.

Chapter 1

*N*ine Ways of Looking at "The Nine"

BEETHOVEN'S SYMPHONIES are both individual pieces of music and imposing cultural monuments. This book is concerned primarily with their musical aspects, but cannot ignore the larger perspective if only because it figures so prominently in both the historical reputation of the music and listeners' expectations. Indeed, it wouldn't be surprising if you first became aware of Beethoven's symphonies as cultural artifacts even before you had experienced them either in concert or through recordings. In short, they are as much talked about as listened to, likely subjects of general discourse in a way that no other classical music, however popular or well known, enjoys.

There is nothing wrong with bringing to the act of listening some understanding of a Beethoven symphony's cultural and historical significance, as long as this doesn't interfere with or replace an attentive, inquisitive engagement with the music itself. It is this extramusical aspect, in fact, that stands in as a kind of surrogate for the one quality that modern audiences can never quite experience the way Beethoven's contemporaries did: the shock of the new, the thrill of hearing a well-understood stylistic vocabulary used in a fresh, sometimes radical way. It pays, then, to spend a little time in considering the many different perspectives from which these works can be viewed from the modern vantage point, two centuries later. Here, then, are nine different ways of looking at a group of works sometimes referred to simply as "The Nine."

Iconic Examples of Musical Romanticism

Though we are technically going through the "postmodern" period in the arts (whatever that means), the reality is that we view most classical music through the lens of nineteenth-century Romanticism. This is because the great works of the Romantic period, by composers such as Tchaikovsky, Brahms, Dvořák, Strauss, Mahler, Bruckner, Schumann, Bizet, Wagner, Verdi, and many others, constitute the bulk of today's active repertoire, and accordingly condition our preferences and expectations. Modern music is deemed "approachable" to the extent that it retains elements understood to be typically Romantic (i.e., emotionally pregnant tunes), while earlier music that anticipates the Romantic style receives greater attention and respect than pieces that fail to show similar progressive tendencies. Beethoven's output, as we will see very shortly, is particularly rich in this area.

Just what does "Romantic" mean? Today, in hindsight, the term is used to represent the opposite of "Classical," and denotes a style in which the spontaneous expression of emotion and the subjective feelings of the artist take precedence over questions of stylistic purity and formal balance. But this gross oversimplification muddles the facts in the worst sort of way. Neither Haydn, nor Mozart, nor Beethoven would have considered their music to be "Classical," but they would have readily acknowledged it "Romantic," as did their contemporaries. In this latter sense, the term means "strongly emotionally affecting," but this usage is so generic as to be also quite unhelpful for our purposes.

Historians, who like to invent tidy theories of periodicity, generally place the dividing line between the Classical and Romantic periods somewhere between Beethoven's death in 1827 and the premiere of Berlioz's *Symphonie fantastique* a few years later. The popularity of the period performance movement, however, which has reclaimed so much worthy Baroque and early Classical period music, has so enlarged our modern perception of the repertoire that identification of Romantic musical elements, if not the start of the actual "period," has been steadily pushed back, at least to Haydn's emotionally flamboyant *Sturm und Drang* (storm and stress) excursion in the late 1760s and early 1770s.

Even the more traditionally minded musical scholars have always had a hard time squaring the view of Beethoven as the last of the great Viennese Classicists with the fact that the first major German Romantic opera, Weber's *Der Freischütz*, had its premiere as early as 1821, more than half a decade before Beethoven's death. In truth, the two periods coexisted side by side for a time, and the move from one to the other was gradual rather than abrupt. So it's much easier and more logical to ignore the question of periodicity, and instead consider qualitative factors. What are the elements in Beethoven's music that influenced later generations of musicians in what we now call the Romantic period?

The first of these isn't really musical at all, but political. Beethoven was a resolute antimonarchist, an ideological supporter of the values of the French Revolution as initially embodied in the person of Napoleon. His Third Symphony, the *Eroica*, is an explicit tribute to those ideals. At a still deeper level, however, works such as the *Eroica*; the *Pastoral* Sixth Symphony's paean to nature; the "rescue" opera *Fidelio*, with its portrait of female courage and fidelity; the *Missa Solemnis*, with its dramatic concluding "prayer for inward and outward peace"; and, above all, the egalitarian Ninth Symphony, with its message that "all men are brothers" speak to one of the linchpins of Romantic thought: the idea of music as a transfiguring moral and ethical force. Even the Fifth Symphony, whose opening motive Beethoven likened to "fate knocking at the door," belongs on this list, at least to the extent that the joyous finale represents an unambiguous victory over the fateful four-note motive unleashed in the first movement.

Beethoven certainly was not the first of the Viennese masters to build into supposedly abstract orchestral music some kind of philosophical program. Haydn, for example, claimed that some of his symphonies illustrated moral or religious principles, but he declined to elaborate with respect to specifics which works these were. In Beethoven's case, we not only have his word about some of the overarching extramusical ideas that run through his symphonies, but the music itself makes this clear and demands that they be taken into account. Romantic composers seized upon this aspect of Beethoven's art—the notion of his music's underlying "program"—with exceptional enthusiasm and interpreted it in different ways.

Here, for example, is what Tchaikovsky had to say about his own Fourth Symphony to his colleague Tanayev:

> In essence my symphony imitates Beethoven's Fifth—in other words, I was not copying its musical ideas, but its basic concept. Do you think that the Fifth Symphony has an underlying program? Not only does it have a program, but in this particular work there can be no question about the effort it makes to find self-expression.

Tchaikovsky certainly was not alone in adopting this view of Beethoven. It was widely shared, even though it fostered some highly divergent opinions.

Consequently, Wagner maintained that after Beethoven the symphony was "dead" because, in choosing to set a text in his Ninth Symphony, Beethoven acknowledged the underlying programmatic basis of modern (that is, Romantic) music generally. Mahler, a bit deeper and more balanced in his thinking in this respect, took Beethoven as his basis for the notion that the symphony "must be the world, it must embrace everything." Here Mahler puts his finger on the exact quality that Beethoven's music had to an unprecedented degree for its time (and ours): a universal, all-encompassing quality that looked beyond conventional notions of "good taste" and compositional correctness to make a statement about the human condition. In the ongoing aesthetic battle between beauty and truth, it is the latter that often seems to gain the upper hand, a fact which Beethoven's detractors were fond of mentioning.

This, combined with his music's extraordinary difficulty and virtuosity, its straining for effect, its disregard for the limitations or prerogatives of performers (such as Beethoven's refusal to give the soloist room to improvise the traditional cadenza in the first movement of his Fifth Piano Concerto), was all new and tremendously exciting. It disgusted more conservative, and, to be frank, less talented composers both in Beethoven's own time and for many decades after his death. From this duality in his character stems the greatest musical battle of the entire nineteenth century: the struggle between the classically oriented "absolutists," whose champion was Brahms, and the proponents of "program" or illustrative music, led by progressive composers Liszt and Wagner (and including Bruckner as "their" symphonist), with both sides claiming to be Beethoven's true heirs.

However, one aspect of Beethoven's art that both sides of this debate wholeheartedly embraced was how, in works such as the *Missa Solemnis*, the Ninth Symphony, and even the late piano sonatas and string quartets, Beethoven turned the concert room into a kind of sacred performance space, a temple dedicated to the religion of music where followers could "worship" through the act of listening. It's a moot point to speculate about the extent to which Beethoven was conscious of this or intended it; his successors saw this quality in his music and embraced it. Henceforth, the Romantic composer—and to a lesser extent the performer—was a high priest of art fulfilling a sacred duty, with the listening public serving as participants in a quasi-religious ritual.

The most extreme manifestation of this secular religion was Wagner's construction of his theater at Bayreuth specifically for the performance of his music dramas; like most ideologies this one has had both benevolent and inimical manifestations. But it all started with Beethoven, and in particular with his symphonies, works which set new standards of seriousness and intensity for what a composer could attempt to express to a mass audience. Abstract instrumental music ceased to be mere amusement: it had become a Big Deal. This above all constitutes Beethoven's legacy to Romanticism, and it's probably fair to say that in this respect his "major" symphonies (nos. 3, 5, 6, 7, and 9) have never been surpassed. Yet despite all this, Beethoven's Romantic side remains but one piece of a larger whole. It is the tension between the Romantic aspect of his art and the Classical approach to form and musical movement through time, described below, that gives his symphonies much of their special expressive potency.

The Apotheosis of the Classical Symphony

The so-called First Viennese School gave us both the masterpieces of the Classical period, and the first works to enjoy an unbroken performance tradition from their first performances to the present in the repertoires of orchestras, chamber ensembles, instrumental soloists, choral societies, and opera companies. Its outstanding members were Haydn, Mozart, and Beethoven, and because the number three has so much resonance, most lists stop there, but two other major composers (one Viennese and one not) deserve to be included—Schubert and Rossini. There is, however, another very good reason that the Big Three dominate our modern perception of the Classical period; Haydn and Mozart knew each other and were in fact best friends, while Beethoven was Mozart's spiritual, and Haydn's actual, student.

More important, all three composers had a very specific conception of what instrumental music should be, one which can best be summed up as "dramatic movement through time." What this means is that a piece of abstract or textless music tells a story in which various characters (themes and motives), representing feelings or emotions, embark on an expressive journey. In short, "stuff happens." These characters interact, develop, switch roles, come and go, combine harmoniously, argue acrimoniously, and follow an overarching plot progression that culminates in a satisfying resolution in which the main players return to their point of origin, usually recognizable but most often changed by their experiences along the way.

The idea of music as a process more or less continually in motion, constantly evolving and changing through the interaction of its various parts, represented a radical break with the prevailing aesthetic of the Baroque period (roughly 1600–1750), which viewed music largely in rhetorical terms—as a type of highly developed discussion. The best-known musical form embodying this style is the fugue, a polyphonic (many-voiced) piece for a fixed number of musical lines or "voices," each of which takes turns presenting and developing the principal musical idea or "subject," first singly and then in combination. Still, it would be incorrect to say that composers in the Classical period rejected the previous period's stance entirely. On the contrary, it was absorbed and incorporated into the new means of thinking about music, becoming one of its many vital components. For example, you will encounter a magnificent fugue in the second movement of Beethoven's Seventh.

The new process characteristic of the Classical period has since become knows as "sonata form," or, more accurately, the "sonata style," as it encompasses whole works, even whole operas, including numerous parts which may or may not use a textbook version of the eponymous form. Another reason to prefer the word "style" is that no Classical period composers knew about anything called "sonata form." They simply wrote music in what was, according to them, the most modern and forward-looking way. The technical terms actually date from the Romantic period.

You may already be familiar with the emphasis on form in the Classical period; it is one of those subjects that comes up constantly in discussions about music in large forms, such as symphonies, concertos, and sonatas. The reason for this is simple: the classical approach to musical shape and structure persisted well beyond the actual period (roughly 1750–1830). It was consciously adopted by most Romantic composers, and has remained vital and important right up to the present day. So, understanding the forms of instrumental music in the Classical period provides a key to almost everything that came later, and it's not nearly as difficult or complicated a subject as you might think, once you know some basic terminology.

The sonata style was largely invented and perfected by Haydn, the greatest musical innovator in history. Its outstanding qualities are:

- the ability to encompass a hitherto unheard of-range of emotional expression within a single movement;
- unprecedented formal coherence, permitting works of greater length and thematic variety;
- extreme flexibility in the handling of musical structure, arising directly out of the diverse nature of the themes themselves;
- basic musical ideas (themes and motives), often of striking outward simplicity, chosen equally for immediacy of effect and long-range developmental potential;
- a genuine feeling of forward progress through time as the music is played, with all of the possibilities for spontaneity and dramatic surprise that this suggests.

As you can see, these qualities are all interrelated to some degree. Most writers on the subject correctly emphasize the importance of tonality, or key, to the proper working of the sonata style, and discussions of a composer's handling of tonality in a movement or over the course of a work can become highly technical and complex. However, the reality from the listener's perspective is that you don't need to know any more about tonality than you need a degree in architecture to understand and appreciate the shape and design of a building. Just as you observe the visible structure of the building, so you hear the form of a piece of music, and tonality merely articulates that form in a way that makes it more readily clear and expressive in fulfillment of the above criteria.

It does this by establishing a main key as "home," the point where the musical journey begins, pausing along the way to

visit subordinate keys. These various stops produce the sensation of "distance" from the home key. Time also passes as the
music travels or "modulates" between the points on each work's
individual musical map. The physical sensation of motion depends
on the composer's ability or desire to make audible the musical
process of leaving home and ultimately returning—most obviously
at three points in a typical movement in sonata form: the very
beginning, the moment of recapitulation (the return to the opening in its original key), and at the very end.

This process of departure and return is what really defines a
movement in "sonata form," one which, as suggested above, falls
naturally into several clearly defined sections:

1. The *exposition*, which contains most of the main thematic
   material of the movement spread out over two *subjects*, one in
   the home or "tonic" key, the next at the first major stopping
   point or subsidiary key, often but not always the *dominant*—
   the key whose own octave scale begins on the fifth note of
   the home key's scale. (I offer these technical terms merely
   so that they will be familiar to you if you see them used; you
   certainly don't have to think about them any further when
   actually listening.) There is no limit to what can go into each
   of these two main subjects; they can have one theme or many,
   long melodies or short motives, in any combination. This is
   because what matters isn't so much the number and size of
   the themes, but rather how securely they define the keys that
   they inhabit. In other words, each subject has both an immediate expressive effect, but also a larger formal function in the
   movement as a whole. This duality makes possible:

2. The *development* section, in which the composer's imagination
   gets to run amok, taking the two subjects through different
   keys, combining themes, introducing new ones, excluding
   some, expanding others—there is almost no limit to what
   can happen in a development section. Some are completely
   episodic—that is, based entirely on new material. Others will

focus only on a tiny piece of original thematic material, subjecting it to the most remarkable transformations. The only challenge the composer must bear in mind is that ultimately, after so much activity and relative instability, the music naturally must return home to provide a satisfying conclusion in the form of:

3. The *recapitulation*, the arrival of which often constitutes one of the more memorable incidents in a sonata-form movement. Note, however, that I did not say "climax." Many formal surprises occur at very soft dynamic levels, in Beethoven no less than in Haydn and Mozart, and the approach to the recapitulation can take many different forms depending, once again, on the nature of the themes and the progress of their prior development. The most important thing to note about the recapitulation is that in order to counterbalance the range of previous activity, all of the themes will be played in (or close to) the home key. This means that the second subject, as well as the transitional ideas or "motion music" that got us there by *modulating* from one key to the next, have to be recomposed in order to remain in place.

In other words, the recapitulation, even when it has the same material as the exposition, presented in the same order (not always the case), will still be somewhat different. The process of returning home invariably changes the themes, sometimes minimally, at other times a great deal. Thus the sonata style is inherently dynamic and evolutionary, and this fact adds further opportunities for dramatic incident, even when the music is most concerned with what may seem at first to be mere repetition of music heard before. In some cases, and quite often in Mozart's music, this modified restatement of the main themes is sufficient to round off the movement and bring it to a satisfying close. Haydn and Beethoven, however, often take the process of development still further in:

4. The *coda*. Many textbook discussions of sonata form dismiss the coda as a sort of appendix, a means of concluding that appears as a sort of afterthought. After all, the music has already reached home through the recapitulation, so while a few more bars might be entertaining and provide a greater feeling of finality, they hardly seem formally necessary. This viewpoint vastly underestimates the importance of the coda in the hands of composers like Haydn and Beethoven. Both reserve some of their finest and most characteristic moments for their codas, and in terms of musical expression they are every bit as important, and often as long as, the other sections of the movement. Indeed, this fourth section is so significant, especially to Beethoven, and its role in the history of symphonic sonata form so interesting that it pays to take a moment and look into it a bit more closely.

Sonata form falls into a category of musical structures known as "binary"—that is, having two parts. You might justifiably feel that this conflicts with the above description of a movement employing this form as having three main sections, but this apparent paradox is very easy to explain. As I just noted, in its simplest sense the musical journey of a typical sonata-form movement involves two processes: the movement away from the home key and the process of return. So the three main sections—exposition, development, and recapitulation—in turn fall into two big halves, the first consisting of the exposition alone (departure), the second containing the rest of the movement (return).

Originally it was customary for both halves of a sonata-form movement to be repeated. There were good practical reasons for this; a repeated exposition allows the listener to become better acquainted with the main thematic material and so to follow its developments and variations later on. The use of repeats obviously doubles the length of movement, thus taking more time, a desirable quality in an era when the pace of life was less hurried and when performers were accustomed to decorating repeats with all kinds of ornamental additions to show off their taste, imagination, and virtuosity. Sometimes composers would write out varied repeats, and performers had the option to observe them or not, but the practice of asking for repeats of both halves of a sonata-form movement persisted at least until the 1790s.

However, once Haydn discovered the potential of goal-directed tonality, the habit of repeating both parts of a movement sometimes became more of a hindrance than a help. In the first place, as the size of symphonic movements expanded, some movements became very, very lengthy. For example, the slow movement of Mozart's Fortieth Symphony in G minor can last as long as fifteen minutes with both halves repeated, which is vastly more than any of the other movements, even with all of their repeats intact. The lopsided (and often boring) result has not fazed performers from the school of "authentic performance practice," who tend to treat all repeats as sacrosanct, even though there is absolutely no evidence of uniformity in their observance.

More important, the second-half repeat in particular tends to contradict the music's strongly directional, goal-oriented argument. Exposition repeats are less controversial for the reasons just mentioned, and also because the music hasn't traveled very far when they happen. But after spending a good deal of time and effort hammering the main key home for the listener, to go back to the beginning of the development section is like being forced to fly from New York to Los Angeles and just before disembarking start over again from Nebraska. The only composer who regularly understood how to make sense of second-half repeats was Haydn, whose sense of dramatic (and particularly comic) timing and surprise in purely instrumental music has never been surpassed.

Eventually, though, even Haydn evidently felt limited by this device, and in eleven of the twelve famous symphonies that he wrote in the mid 1790s for his concerts in London (nos. 93–104), he dropped the second-half repeat in their first movements. This allowed him to continue to develop the music right up to a single, emphatic ending. But he didn't stop there. Instead of the usual repeat, Haydn made up for the loss by adding a large coda that functions almost like a second development section. He understood that a sudden dramatic surprise in the form of a harmonic digression just before the music's final arrival home could actually enhance the listener's feeling of satisfaction at the concluding moments. Beethoven seized this concept with extraordinary relish. None of his symphonies ask for second-half repeats in their sonata-form opening movements, and in the Fifth and Seventh particularly, he created codas of truly colossal emotional power and impact.

So when I say that Beethoven's works in the genre represent the "apotheosis of the classical symphony," it's for this reason: after 1800 only Beethoven truly understood the potential of music as purposeful dramatic action that his predecessors Haydn and Mozart had exploited so masterfully, and only he took this principal to the next level. After Beethoven there was no significant further progress in this area; composers either wrote music along similar lines or they did not, but if they did, then it was Beethoven whose work served as the highest and best example of what they were trying to achieve. Later figures as diverse as Brahms, Mahler, Dvořák, Tchaikovsky, and Nielsen actually did find their own personal paths to this Beethovenian idea—perhaps equaling but never surpassing his position at the pinnacle of symphonic thought.

The Symphony as Popular Music

It goes without saying that any work requiring a large orchestra for performance also presupposes a large audience, if only for the simple reason that it takes a certain number of paying listeners to offset the cost of assembling an orchestra in the first place. Concerts in Beethoven's day were very long and highly varied. They often included concertos, chamber works, keyboard solos, vocal pieces, improvisations, and choral works in every conceivable proportion. Audiences participated actively, much as they do at jazz or rock concerts today, applauding individual movements, particularly noteworthy themes, instrumental effects, or solo licks.

Frankly, it sounds like everyone had rather more fun than at typical classical music events than we do now; we are still stuck, unfortunately, with the sanctimonious remnants of the Romantic "music as religion" philosophy that Beethoven himself, perhaps unwittingly, fostered.

Main concert attractions, without exception, were instrumental and vocal soloists. They commanded the highest fees (especially the singers), brought in the largest public, served as fodder for juicy gossip—much of which went on during the concert, while the music was playing—and accordingly enjoyed celebrity status. In this respect, very little has changed from Beethoven's day to ours, but one thing markedly different is the role of the symphony in the program. The very word "symphony" was used synonymously with the more frequent "overture," and that latter term points to the music's original function. Symphonies served as introductions, interludes, and conclusions, often being played with their movements broken up and spread around the concert as necessary. It was only very gradually that the symphony itself became the highpoint of the evening, and for that Haydn and Beethoven were entirely responsible.

This particular story begins in the mid-eighteenth century, when Haydn was engaged to run the musical establishment of the noble Esterházy family. A dream job from a composer's point of view, Haydn's employers hired a private orchestra containing some of the finest players in Europe, and then turned him loose on it. Symphonies were, unusually for the time, a preferred form of entertainment because they permitted Haydn to show off the gifts of the entire very expensive, deluxe ensemble to his employer. The fame of both the Esterházy orchestra and the works that Haydn wrote for it soon became so widely known that the composer began to receive commissions from abroad to write symphonies. Once again, Haydn was lucky in that he had permission to accept these offers. They were viewed, in the most enlightened way, as bringing further admiration and respect on the high standard of musical culture prevailing at the house of Esterházy.

Haydn's last twenty-two symphonies, nos. 82–104, were all composed to foreign commissions, either from Paris or London. Haydn never actually went to Paris, but he did spend several seasons in London in the mid-1790s, where he secured his personal fortune and caused a sensation with the music-loving public. The main attractions at his concerts were the twelve so-called London Symphonies, already mentioned—works which set entirely new standards for formal inventiveness, colorful orchestration, tuneful appeal, and expressive depth. They were popular hits, not just among the concertgoing public, but also as played at home in arrangements for piano or chamber ensembles. In Haydn's hands, the symphony came of age as the grandest and most serious of orchestral compositions, just as he single-handedly elevated the string quartet to the pinnacle of chamber music.

Beethoven, as Haydn's difficult pupil, understood exactly what his teacher had accomplished. It's probably fair to say that Beethoven suffered from a double inferiority complex during his formative years. He wanted desperately to write music like Mozart (as everyone who understood his achievements did), but he was temperamentally much better suited to Haydn's style. This was obviously a problem while Haydn was still active, but by 1803 Haydn had retired to live quietly in a suburb of Vienna until his death in 1809, having composed no new symphonies after 1795. It's an interesting coincidence that Beethoven's *Eroica* Symphony, in some ways his musical declaration of independence, dates precisely from the summer of 1803.

Of course there were many other composers writing symphonies at the time, but one of the most fascinating things about the so-called First Viennese School of Haydn, Mozart, and Beethoven, is that they seemed fully aware of their own musical relationship to each other, and of their corporate identity as the best composers of their day. This quiet certainty may not have been widely shared, but it's impossible to study the friendship between Haydn and Mozart, and later Beethoven's view of them both, without coming to this conclusion. Beethoven's initial obnoxious attitude toward Haydn, the obvious product of jealousy and insecurity, gradually turned to adulation as soon as he found his own style and realized that he had nothing to fear from being compared to his illustrious mentor (more on this in the discussion of the Seventh Symphony).

Beethoven took from Haydn the notion of the symphony as popular entertainment, a work that could form the centerpiece of a long concert program, and which, like a Shakespeare play, could contain elements that appealed to all strata of society. Mozart, at the very end of his life, had achieved something very similar in his opera *The Magic Flute*, and all of these works together point to a seismic shift in the social dynamics of musical culture. To put it succinctly, the aristocratic old order was passing away, and as Haydn discovered in London, a new audience for music was growing among the prosperous middle class of industrialists, professionals, and entrepreneurs, a class to which he himself belonged.

Beethoven was ahead of his time in following this trend, no doubt as a result of his revolutionary, egalitarian ideals and distaste for the aristocracy in general. It won't do to press this point too far; after all, Beethoven was for most of his adult life supported by direct stipend from the Viennese nobility, and one of his best friends and supporters was Archduke Rudolf (of the "Archduke" Trio and dedicatee of the *Missa Solemnis*). Nevertheless, with the benefit of hindsight we can see that Beethoven's symphonies ultimately captured the imagination of this new audience in a way that no other composer quite managed. Musically speaking, he did it in several ways that are worth mentioning briefly here.

The first of these was the replacement of the traditional minuet in the usual multimovement sonata scheme with a scherzo, which means "joke." Like so many musical inventions, this one was pioneered by Haydn, but Beethoven's ratification of the practice made the scherzo the standard dance-type movement in most instrumental music. Both are usually composed in 3/4 time, like a waltz, but whereas the minuet is slowish and dignified, the scherzo is quicker and more prone to rhythmic games. More to the point, the minuet was the aristocratic dance *par excellence*, and although

Beethoven didn't abandon it entirely (the Eighth Symphony has one), his preference for the scherzo was a major factor in removing aristocratic associations from the sphere of instrumental music.

This mattered from a sociological point of view because one of the factors that counted in Beethoven's favor, particularly as the nineteenth century wore on, was the fact that he spent his life as a freelance composer. No one better understood the popular style than did Haydn, but his life in service to the Esterházy family led to his being regarded as a servant, a lackey held in lower esteem by subsequent generations than he ever was by his employers, who revered him deeply. His willingness to work within the system was regarded as a character flaw, one which must necessarily have been reflected as a certain shallowness or frivolity in his music. A composer of independent mind such as Beethoven, and to a lesser degree, Mozart, not only wrote for the nascent middle classes, he was seen as a proud member himself, a musical genius who was also "one of us."

These (strictly speaking) extramusical considerations matter hugely in assessing a composer's historical reputation for the simple reason that people often make up their minds about whether or not to listen and to spend time with any piece of music before having heard a note of it, or at best on superficial acquaintance. They come to it with a range of preconceived ideas, and unless the music is truly dreadful or off-putting they usually listen in such a way that any initial biases or assumptions are confirmed by the experience. The fact is that abstract instrumental music will always "mean" whatever the individual listener wants it to, and all of us are naturally conditioned by our own beliefs and expectations.

That said, in Beethoven's time popular music consisted, just as it does today, primarily of songs and dance tunes (including marches); Beethoven's symphonies are full of them. The second subject of his Second Symphony's first movement is a march; the second movement of the *Eroica*, its most famous part, is a funeral march, while the finale is based on a folklike dance tune that he reused multiple times: In his ballet *The Creatures of Prometheus*, as well as in the *Eroica* Variations for solo piano. The Fifth Symphony is full of marchlike music, and the Seventh was called by Wagner the "apotheosis of the dance," while the march variation for tenor solo in the finale of the Ninth Symphony is rightly famous. Beethoven's chamber works also employ plenty of this sort of music, but seldom to the same extent as do the symphonies and other orchestral works.

Alongside this popular treatment of rhythm comes an equally popular use of melody. This was a quality that Beethoven worked at throughout his life. He was not a natural tunesmith, as were Mozart, Schubert, or Dvorák. Beethoven hammered his melodies into their final shape over a process of laborious revision and, as often as not, simplification. He needed tunes that had three basic qualities: uniqueness, the capability of being developed, and at the same time, almost primeval memorability. His sketchbooks are full of examples of his struggles to shape the right thematic material, and the number of tunes and motives that even people with little or no knowledge of classical music instantly recognize is a tribute to his success.

No other composer even comes close to matching Beethoven in this "populist" quality. Furthermore, this fact goes hand in hand with the remarks at the start of this chapter about the Romantic period's need for a repertoire specifically tailored to the emerging view of music as a kind of secular religion, one particularly suited to Europe's increasingly large, culturally enlightened middle classes. In sum, even after the shock of their more radical features has inevitably worn off, when it comes to Beethoven's symphonies familiarity does not breed contempt. They acquired "classic" status and with it an unprecedented mass appeal, a truly remarkable phenomenon given their size and sophistication.

Hallmarks of German Nationalism

The previous discussion of Beethoven as a "popular" composer is inextricably bound with his place in the most powerful and, eventually, pernicious ideological current in the entire nineteenth century: nationalism. Historians have written exhaustively of the rise of German nationalism, a complex topic that forms part of what was later defined in academic circles as "the German Question": How did such a highly cultured society become the willing tool of Nazi fascism? Believe it or not, music plays a significant role in this discussion, as do many other aspects of German culture.

For example, historian George L. Mosse, in his excellent study *The Nationalization of the Masses: Political Symbolism and Mass Movements in Germany from the Napoleonic Wars through the Third Reich*, traces the role of singing societies and other performing arts institutions in creating a cohesive cultural identity for a nation which, prior to unification in 1871, lacked central political organization. In short, while the neighboring French had a long history of statehood, for much of the nineteenth century German-speaking peoples experienced nationhood through language and culture rather than allegiance to a particular monarch, government, or means of political organization.

Music loomed large in this process not only because of mass participation in its performance (remember, in the days before recordings, the only way to hear it outside of a formal concert situation was to play it or sing it yourself), but also because abstract instrumental music was vague enough in content to be the perfect vehicle to embody such intangible qualities such as "the spirit of the nation," and other similar constructs. From the foregoing discussion of Beethoven's special attributes it's easy to see how his public works, the symphonies and concertos (and his single opera), came to have a special significance in German lands. That he was also one of the most highly revered composers internationally didn't hurt either for a nation in search of both self-respect and a sense of identity.

In its original and mostly benign form, the musical wing of German cultural nationalism consisted of a reaction against the dominance of the Italians as singers, instrumentalists, and, above all, opera composers. In Beethoven's day the rising star in the operatic firmament was Rossini, whose music took Vienna by storm and made Beethoven extremely angry. German composers, Beethoven among them, saw little choice in stemming the Italian tide—tuneful, flashy, and resolutely entertaining—than to take a stand for "higher," more serious cultural values and specialize in formally sophisticated instrumental forms. In this they had two excellent historical precedents: Haydn, whose fame during his life-time rested largely on his instrumental works, (never mind that he could hardly be called "German" in the late-nineteenth-century sense), and Mozart, whose operas demonstrated the greater degree of polish that a genius in the purely instrumental realm could bring to the genre.

Of course, there is nothing indisputably "German" about Beethoven's musical technique in either a political or nationalistic sense. However, at a time when the language of the aristocracy was French, and the language of both music and the most popular oper-atic composers was Italian, Beethoven's works easily came to rep-resent the highest and best of what the German spirit had to offer, and stood proud against all challengers. Their propaganda value in this respect cannot be overestimated. It was a performance of *Fidelio* that Wagner later recalled as one of the seminal experiences of his musical life. The Ninth Symphony, played by the Berlin Phil-harmonic under its conductor Wilhelm Furtwängler, became Nazi Germany's cultural calling card (recordings are still available). It was the same Ninth Symphony under Leonard Bernstein that accompanied the fall of the Berlin wall, while decades earlier the *Egmont* Overture served as a heroic funeral tribute to the Israeli athletes killed by terrorists at the 1972 Munich Olympics.

Whether used for good or ill, and despite inroads made by works such as Mahler's *Resurrection* Symphony, Beethoven's symphonies remain the pieces that both musicians and states-men reach for to celebrate significant political events. Their iconic status in Germany is matched only perhaps by the operas of Verdi in Italy, and to a lesser degree by the music of Sibelius in Finland, Elgar in England, and Copland in the United States. This widespread acceptance was not necessarily an unmixed blessing; it forced later German composers to evaluate their music not just in terms of its absolute quality, but also according to a very nebulous and subjective standard of cultural purity.

Nationalism, particularly in the latter half of the nineteenth century, went hand in hand with racism, social Darwinism, eugenics, and other equally vile ideas. The result was, in musical terms, a particularly poisonous intellectual brew that, to the extent that it led to a rejection of foreign or non-Germanic influences, unquestionably did German composers more harm than good. Ironically, while reverence for Beethoven's example and respect for German culture served as an example to symphonists in France, Russia, the Slavic lands, and Scandinavia, it tended to dry up potential sources of inspiration available to German composers. The result was that the best of them, such as Wagner and Strauss, turned away from symphonic composition entirely, and even geniuses such as Brahms approached the task with the greatest trepidation.

Of course, none of this artistic downside was Beethoven's fault, and there's no question that nationalist prejudice and exclusivity stood in stark opposition to the values of egalitarianism and universal brotherhood that he so vocally espoused. Beethoven the "pure" German was, musically speaking, an eclectic. He was castigated for these qualities in his own lifetime by those such as composer Louis Spohr, who questioned his sense of beauty (but performed him anyway), and even much later by aestheticians such as Viennese critic Eduard Hanslick, who declared the finale of the Ninth Symphony an uncomfortable hybrid. Later composers who emulated his example in this respect, such as Mahler, incurred the double opprobrium in Germany of being both eclectic *and* foreign. The legacy of Beethoven as a specifically German composer is thus decidedly equivocal.

From a purely musical point of view, Beethoven bequeathed to his nation an unparalleled artistic legacy, but its impact on German culture when co-opted by the forces of nationalism could not, by definition, remain entirely beneficial. The evidence of this is indisputable. After Brahms's death in 1896, there are no German symphonists of worldwide repute. However, in the rest of the world Beethoven's legacy produced an explosion of fine composers working in the symphonic field, an impact that continues to be felt to the present day just about everywhere—except in Germany, where no modern composer has taken up Beethoven's symphonic challenge to general international acclaim.

Linchpins of the Modern Repertoire

The symphony orchestra in its modern form is a relatively recent invention, developing simultaneously on both sides of the Atlantic. You may hear claims, particularly from Germany, that ensembles such as the Leipzig Gewandhaus Orchestra and the Staatskapelle Dresden (Dresden State Orchestra) have been around for centuries, but leaving aside the understandable obsession with pedigree that ignores historical differences in ensemble size, composition, and repertoire, the fact is that the world's two oldest, independently constituted, continuously performing orchestras are probably the Vienna and New York Philharmonics, both of which got going in 1842. Everyone else came later, and you will note that even these two venerable institutions postdate Beethoven's death by a decade and a half. The most active age of orchestral formation came in the thirty-year period between about 1880 and 1910, when many of the ensembles that we still know today were founded.

In Beethoven's own time, concert orchestras were what we would call "pick up" ensembles, consisting primarily of musicians playing regularly in opera houses or theaters, traveling freelancers, performers in service to various noble families (woodwinds especially), and, in the provinces, students, semiprofessionals, and volunteers. Trumpets and timpani, when required, were often provided on loan from the military. These groups were assembled by an impresario, a touring artist, or a composer, who was responsible for all of the financial details—hiring a hall, copying music, engaging guest artists, marketing and advertising, selling tickets, and ultimately paying the players. Composers and solo performers all had to have this basic business acumen, and as soon as the concert or series of concerts was over, the orchestra disbanded.

You can readily imagine that under this system, rehearsal time tended to be minimal. There's a famous letter from Haydn requesting that his latest symphonies, on account of their many special and difficult instrumental effects, be rehearsed at least once before the actual performance. Beethoven's concerts have thus come down in history as famously error ridden. From the orchestra that broke down during the *Eroica* and had to start over, to his podium antics as the world's first (and hopefully only) deaf conductor, a great many of his premiers must have been tragicomic events. This does not mean that the overall standard of playing was poor, but it does suggest that concert orchestras could hardly have enjoyed the kind of corporate identity and discipline that we have since come to expect and demand as a matter of course.

All the more reason, then, that these quirky, difficult, undeniably brilliant but eccentric works would make excellent calling cards to advertise the skill of the nineteenth century's newly constituted full-time orchestras. Bear in mind also that most people's experience of these works came not from hearing them in concert, but from playing through piano or chamber reductions suitable for use at home. The rise of the modern symphony orchestra thus occurred exactly in tandem with the widespread international dissemination of Beethoven's symphonic works in the decades immediately following his death. Audiences wanted to hear them live, and orchestras needed both new works as well as a repertoire of certified but not excessively old-fashioned classics guaranteed to sell tickets. It was a match made in heaven.

Orchestras today, with the possible exception of the Vienna Philharmonic, seldom make Beethoven their proprietary calling cards. Later composers, Mahler in particular, have written larger, more virtuosic symphonies that give our technically superb players a more extensive workout. But the Beethoven symphonies remain the ultimate test on a much deeper level, of ensemble, musicality, profundity of expression, concentration, and intensity.

An orchestra that plays Beethoven well can truly be said to have "arrived" at a certain level of artistic maturity. Those that cannot will never enjoy the acclaim accorded the world's best ensembles. The nine symphonies are no longer novelties; rather, they have become compulsory, the foundation on which an orchestra's reputation is built.

The same observations apply to the rise of the conductor. Although Beethoven himself conducted the premiers of his symphonies, the orchestra actually followed the first violinist, more or less. Conducting per se was limited to keeping everyone together and ensuring a clean ensemble. It was never the job of the conductor to impose his personal concept of corporate sonority and style on his unruly mob of freelancers, an impossible task anyway given prevailing conditions. Nevertheless, the rhythmic difficulties of his symphonies, and the problems of balance and coordination that they present, demanded a strong guiding hand at the podium. Accordingly, the rise of permanent orchestras meant the rise of permanent conductors, and Beethoven was the composer on whose back most built their reputations. This remained largely true until slightly after the mid-twentieth century.

The deaths in the 1950s of Arturo Toscanini and Wihelm Furtwängler, and the passings about a decade later of Otto Klemperer and George Szell, signaled the end of the era in which conductors linked their artistic identities primarily to their interpretations of Beethoven's symphonies. The rise of "guest conductors," of orchestras with fifty-two-week seasons run by music directors obligated to conduct only a quarter of the year's concerts, has limited the ability and, more important, the desire, of conductors to impose their will on an orchestra to the extent that it matters in playing Beethoven, whether live or on recordings. In a very real sense, we live in a time where conditions are quite similar, through for different reasons, to those prevailing in Beethoven's own day.

The most significant modern twist on the continuing saga of Beethoven's status as the linchpin of the modern repertoire stems from a simple fact: most orchestras are technically better at what they do than most conductors, even though conductors take all the credit for whatever occurs when they happen to be waving their hands about. This makes the conductor far less necessary in his or her most basic function: ensuring correct playing of the printed music. Beethoven presents few technical difficulties to today's first- and second-tier ensembles, and for this reason conductors sometimes are reluctant to spend valuable time rehearsing his music in the same way that, say, an unfamiliar modern work might require. In short, he has become a victim of overfamiliarity.

There are exceptions. Leonard Bernstein confirmed his status as a "grand old man" with his second Beethoven cycle (on Deutsche Grammophon) featuring the Vienna Philharmonic. At the very end of his life, German conductor Günter Wand returned to his roots, focusing on the core German repertoire with his North German Radio (NDR) Symphony Orchestra, leaving behind a magnificent Beethoven cycle for RCA as its centerpiece. Daniel Barenboim, with his Staatskapelle Berlin (Warner/Teldec), took an approach similar to Bernstein's, certifying his credentials in the German classics with one of the finest Beethoven cycles in modern times. Finnish conductor Osmo Vänskä and the Minnesota Orchestra (BIS Records) undertook to prove their excellence the old-fashioned way with a superb series of Beethoven symphony recordings, while Paavo Järvi has done the same with the Deutsche Kammerorchester Bremen (RCA).

The presence of so many recordings of Beethoven symphonies, dozens of complete cycles and hundreds of individual performances, however, tends to blur the distinctions between artists, and makes it more difficult to get noticed in this repertoire unless, like Mikhail Pletnev with the Russian National Orchestra (Deutsche Grammophon), the conductor chooses to be willfully perverse, damn the consequences. There are many conductors, some only fitfully responsive to the full range of Beethoven's language, who have recorded multiple cycles, or partial cycles. These include such major names as Herbert von Karajan, Georg Solti, Karl Böhm, Bernard Haitink, Kurt Masur, Bruno Walter, and

Claudio Abbado. To this should be added the deluge of "historical" broadcast or pirate recordings of live performances by famous conductors of the past.

So while there's certainly no dearth of excellence or character in Beethoven performance today, it can be hard to spot amid the average efforts, most of which offer a high level of technical quality and at least tastefully safe interpretive parameters. However, despite the danger of drowning in a glut of the merely good, at the end of the day the musical world invariably still sits up and takes notice whenever an artist comes along with something new and special to say in Beethoven. Noteworthy performances of his symphonies (and string quartets, and piano sonatas) still represent the ultimate achievement that sustains a musician's claim to greatness. And if circumstances at present make rising to the challenge more difficult than formerly, then the triumph of our finest artists will only shine brighter as a result.

Test Cases for Historical Performance Practice

The very notion of "historical performance practice" is, by and large, a matter of conjecture, and the idea that it somehow brings with it a measure of "authenticity" is sheer nonsense. We have no precise idea what performances in Beethoven's day sounded like. Furthermore, as the previous discussion makes very clear, much of what we do know unquestionably falls into the category of things that no sane performers today would ever want to duplicate, and no modern audience would tolerate. That said, the historically informed performance (HIP, for short) movement has been, on the whole, a good thing for classical music, not because it uses gut strings, valveless brass, and timpani with wooden sticks, but because it has forced musicians to take a good hard look at the scores and start from scratch.

Ironically, to the extent that the HIP movement's success has been the degree to which it has adopted a literal approach to the printed text, this is perhaps the most inauthentic perspective it would be possible to imagine. In Beethoven's day, performers ruled.

Melodic lines were ornamented, multimovement works might be broken up and played in independent bits, have their movements rearranged, and in general be treated with a disdain for the composer's intentions that modern musicians couldn't duplicate if they wanted to. Standards of everything, from playing technique, quality of instrumental construction, composition of the orchestra, the role of the conductor (if any), pitch, and tuning, varied widely from place to place.

The HIP movement arose as a practical performance corollary to the discipline of musicology, which got started in the nineteenth century, largely in Germany and France. Complete editions of past masters such as Bach, Handel, Palestrina, and Rameau were published for the first time. Major composers, such as Brahms and Saint-Saëns, participated in this process as editors and advisors, and by the turn of the twentieth century, early music groups began playing on old-style instruments and experimenting with hypothetical approximations of period sound. In the English-speaking world, the great pioneer of early music performance was Arnold Dolmetsch, and many music lovers will also know the name of keyboard artist Wanda Landowska, who revived interest in the harpsichord in the period following World War I.

So the HIP movement as such is not new. What transformed it from a sort of minority cult born in the nineteenth-century academic ghetto into a mainstream enterprise was a combination of two factors. The first of these was, and remains, the oversupply of conservatories churning out musician who need work. Early music ensembles tend to be small, and from an organizational standpoint easier (meaning less expensive) to assemble. They are mobile, and easily adaptable to nontraditional performance spaces such as churches, meeting halls, and smaller rooms.

The second factor was the classical recording mania that accompanied the creation of the compact disc and the acquisition of the major classical labels by large corporate conglomerates with deep pockets. Cheaper to record than large modern orchestras, while offering new-sounding interpretations of tried and true classics, and particularly of minor or neglected works by major Baroque composers, HIP seemed tailor-made to the recording explosion that took place in the 1980s and '90s. In England, for example, the Academy of Ancient Music, the English Concert, the Hanover Band, the Orchestra of the Age of Enlightenment, and other similar groups shared personnel but changed names depending on who led them and what label recorded them.

This process came to a climax in 1991, the bicentenary of Mozart's death, when the glut of supposedly "authentic" recordings of the hundreds of unimportant works that Mozart churned out as a child prodigy reached absolutely ridiculous proportions. Baroque and classical composers were nothing if not prolific, and while plenty of forgettable hackwork has now been recorded, the process has, more importantly, uncovered large numbers of otherwise forgotten or neglected gems by figures such as Zelenka, Veracini, Campra, Charpentier, Rosetti, Hummel, Witt, and Kalliwoda, to list only a random few. The subsequent implosion of the classical recording industry in the late 1990s stemmed the tide of major label releases, but not of new early music productions, which remain cost-effective ways to explore the bottomless pit of yet-to-be-recorded seventeenth- through nineteenth-century music.

If some of this seems to you only tangentially related to art and overly concerned with economics, you're quite right. The Achilles' heel of the HIP movement has always been the fact that its validity rests not so much on doing something that is "authentic," but in creating jobs for itinerant musicians, and consequently in defining historical correctness as whatever sounds as different as possible from modern standards. Mind you, I am not trying to be cynical. This does not mean that there aren't some splendid artists and ensembles making fabulous music among adherents of the HIP philosophy. My point is cautionary: Don't fall for the movement's PR. Judge each performance on its own musical merits. Above all, don't accept the notion that scholarly rectitude inherently leads to higher standards, and better or more perceptive interpretations. Ugly is as ugly sounds.

The record of the HIP movement in Beethoven has been decidedly mixed for a number of reasons. Period performance specialists have been most successful in music of the Baroque and earlier, perhaps because with only a few exceptions there was no established modern tradition in that repertoire, and also because, let's face it, their approach really does suit the music. Problems begin to arise, however, as soon as these same musicians venture into the late Classical and Romantic periods. In a very real sense, the modern orchestra is the creation of this particular repertoire, and ideally fitted to it. Much of this music has enjoyed an unbroken history of performance stretching back for several centuries. This tradition is not something that can be dismissed lightly by academic speculation.

So what, then, are the pros and cons in comparing "original" and "modern" instrument performances, keeping in mind, of course—particularly when it comes to the strings—that most modern instruments are in fact originals (think Stradivarius or Guarneri), while most "original" instruments are actually precision-tooled modern copies? Consider the following topics: dynamics, sonority, and tempo.

Dynamics

There has always been a tendency for modern orchestras to handle music of the Classical period with kid gloves, to refuse to play a true fortissimo, or even use the full forces at their disposal. This is because orchestras in the Romantic period tend to be so much larger and louder, and the Classical period is viewed in contrast as a time of "elegance" and "restraint," which is unfortunately often synonymous with interpretive tedium. The HIP movement has demonstrated very persuasively that it is far more exciting to hear a smaller ensemble playing flat out, with a wide dynamic range and fortissimos that push the instruments to their limits, than it is to hear a bigger group trying to be cute and dainty.

Additionally, Classical-period dynamics tend to be "terraced"— that is, with clear gradations between loud and soft. Crescendos and diminuendos, those gradually swelling and receding dynamic inflections, are used far less frequently than in later music—which hasn't prevented modern conductors from adding them anyway. The result is a smoother, less eruptive musical surface, and this can only compromise the drama and surprise inherent in so many Classical works. One of the signal achievements of the HIP movement, then, has been to insist on playing the music's original dynamics, and making their range from soft to loud as wide as the instruments can accommodate.

You would think that this point should be obvious, and of course the best modern performances don't fall into this particular trap. However, because Classical period works usually appear on the first half of a typical program and are technically easier to play than big Romantic concertos and symphonies, they are often underrehearsed and flabbily played. One telling sign of inadequate preparation is a lack of attention to dynamics and accents, for while Classical works may be not be technically challenging compared to later pieces, they are certainly not easier to play superbly. In fact, they can be much more difficult because they have so little musical padding, relatively speaking.

Thus, the argument in favor of the HIP position isn't just a vote for a particular performance style. It also contains the universal truth that specialization, generous rehearsal time, and familiarity with the music contribute to excellent results. Of course, all nine of Beethoven's symphonies are so well known that most modern orchestral musicians can play them at a very high level of finish, so we must be careful in framing generalizations. Still, the combination of stylistic approach and interpretive philosophy in HIP performances leads to a treatment of dynamics which, if not necessarily "better" all of the time, is seldom unpersuasive or unidiomatic.

Sonority

Sonority is a large and complex topic, involving matters such as sectional balances as well as both individual and group sonorities. The most obvious starting point is the string section. In no area of the HIP movement is there more nonsense being spouted than in the area of string technique. Current theory posits, without a shred of firm historical evidence, that orchestral string players avoided the use of vibrato almost entirely. Vibrato is that tiny rocking of the left hand that gives individual notes a warm, vocal quality, which has been the primary goal of instrumental technique from the dawn of time right through to the present. The biggest proponent of this fiction has been the conductor Roger Norrington, whose statements on this subject reveal an odd combination of opportunism, historical selectivity, and inconsistency.

Vibrato in an orchestral context cannot be heard as a distinct variance in pitch. Indeed, applied correctly in any but the most exaggerated way, whether by soloists or large string sections, it can barely be heard at all. In the orchestra, it subtly aids in creating an even blending of timbres, focuses intonation, and adds color and variety of texture. Strings that play without vibrato often sound thin and out of tune. However, not all HIP practitioners abjure vibrato. Nikolaus Harnoncourt, for example, perhaps the movement's most important pioneer, accepts its natural presence in the Romantic orchestra, while preferring less vibrato in music of earlier periods. This is not new. Leonard Bernstein, for example, was demonstrating much the same thing in his Young People's Concerts back in the 1960s.

You may very well hear claims that vibrato is "impure," that its presence "clogs" textures and produces a "muddy" ensemble, or that there is a big difference between modern, "continuous" vibrato and an earlier, "ornamental" type. This is mostly just self-serving propaganda. There is no such thing as "continuous" vibrato in the sense that followers of the HIP school often suggest. Furthermore, the more significant determinant of clarity and balance between orchestral sections, not surprisingly, is the size of the orchestra and the resonance of the performance space. All other considerations are secondary. In this respect, it's probably safe to say that neither modern nor HIP performances do justice to much of the Classical repertoire.

We know for a fact that Haydn, Mozart, and Beethoven loved working with large orchestras. The band that premiered Haydn's last "London" symphonies, for example, numbered some sixty players in a hall that seated about eight hundred. Compare this to a typical modern performance of a classical symphony, using about forty players in rooms with a capacity upwards of two thousand, and you can clearly understand how poorly the music is being served. Haydn or Mozart, seeing the capacity of, say, Carnegie Hall, would have demanded an orchestra of close to a hundred players, exactly what we use now in large Romantic works. If this means doubling or trebling the winds and timpani, as many orchestras do in Beethoven's Ninth Symphony, then so be it.

Period instrument performances then, often with ensembles much smaller than thirty or forty players, can be even worse than modern groups when heard live, but they can conceal this defect very effectively on recordings. The comparative wimpiness of Classical period music played with restricted dynamics by reduced modern orchestras in vast halls, as compared with the bold, crisp, snappy timbres of many period instrument groups heard in smaller, more acoustically flattering spaces, offers telling evidence of the critical role that recording technology has played in spreading the HIP gospel. I have to say quite frankly that I have always been more impressed by period instrument groups on disc than in concert, and this is just the opposite of my experience with conventional orchestras, which (at least in Romantic music) always sound far better live.

Given the above generalizations, you may also find it curious that the recorded evidence reveals quite clearly that HIP ensembles enjoy no consistent advantage when it comes to textural transparency and just balances between sections. Indeed, you will never hear woodwind parts rendered with more clarity in Classical period works than in the Haydn, Mozart, and Beethoven recordings of Otto Klemperer, one of the grandest practitioners working in the early twentieth-century German tradition. This was entirely by design, not happenstance. If conductors and players value clarity of texture, then that is what you will hear. If they do not, then the kind of instruments or performance practice matters not one whit.

Another area in which both modern and HIP ensembles routinely fall short concerns their handling of bass lines. At the risk of oversimplification, it can be said that Classical period music really does consist mostly of a top and a bottom with everyone else filling in, and it's not unusual for that bottom (that is, cellos, basses, bassoons, or bass trombone) to get the tune. Composers of the day often used a very large number of basses, proportionately many more than would be typical today even if we acknowledge that the carrying power of the older instruments was somewhat less. They also had no qualms about doubling bass parts using any other wind instruments of the correct range that happened to be available.

Today, on the other hand, you will never see Classical period works played with full bass sections (eight to ten players). Larger chamber orchestras may have half that number, and period instrument groups are often even smaller. This practice is not only unhistorical; it really does play havoc with the composer's intended balances. In the following discussions, this issue will come up repeatedly, because Beethoven often does wonderful and interesting things with his bass lines, and he intends that you hear them. It's really rather amazing that so few conductors have given this question the attention that it deserves (Charles Mackerras is one, and we will discuss his solution with respect to the Fifth Symphony in considering that work's orchestration).

However, when it comes to sonority modern orchestras enjoy a very real advantage over HIP groups in one respect; they have the best players using the finest quality instruments. At the beginning of the authentic instrument revolution, in the 1960s and '70s, there was no question that much of the "radical" nature of period-instrument sound stemmed from the scruffy playing of unfamiliar or awkwardly made replicas of primitive instruments. Once again, recordings reveal quite clearly a steady advance in refinement and tone quality as HIP specialists have mastered their craft, and as the movement has attracted top-quality talent. In short, the better the player, the less "authentic" he is likely to sound.

This same timbral divide used to characterize (and sometimes still does) orchestras in Eastern and Western Europe (as well as the Americas). I vividly recall an interview with a noted Czech conductor in which I asked him if there was any truth to the notion that the Czech Philharmonic, one of the world's greatest and most distinctive orchestras, had lost much of its characteristically lean and wiry sound over the course of the 1980s and '90s. He replied that in his view the school of playing remained much the same, but with the collapse of communism the musicians simply had access to better quality instruments and accessories and thus sounded smoother.

In sum, an audible qualitative gap often remains between the best modern and HIP groups, and it is perhaps for this reason that the most successful period-style Beethoven cycles remain those played on modern instruments. This, for example, is how Nikolaus Harnoncourt recorded his Beethoven cycle (with the Chamber Orchestra of Europe, using old-style brass), and the same holds true for the more or less HIP-influenced performances of Charles Mackerras (Royal Liverpool Philharmonic, Scottish Chamber Orchestra, Philharmonia Orchestra), David Zinman (Tonhalle Orchester of Zurich), Thomas Dausgaard (Swedish Chamber Orchestra), Osmo Vänskä (Minnesota Orchestra), Paavo Järvi (Deutsche Kammerphilharmonie Bremen), and Bernard Haitink (London Symphony Orchestra). Even Roger Norrington's Beethoven conducting, distressingly crude and clumsy with the scrappy London Classical Players, improved beyond recognition when he had an experienced German ensemble under his baton (the SWR Radio Symphony Orchestra).

Tempo

This one's easy: HIP performances are often quicker than modern ones. There are several reasons for this. First, smaller ensembles often compensate for lack of tonal heft by increasing speed and, theoretically, excitement. Second, the evidence of historical recordings shows that tempos seem to have slowed down some-what over the course of the twentieth century, perhaps because of the emphasis on technical perfection and a rich surface sonority. Of course, this doesn't mean that the quicker tempos characteristic of the early 1900s were "normal." For all we know, they may have been slower a few decades earlier; we have no audible evidence one way or the other.

The differences between HIP and modern interpretations regarding tempo are most often discernable in slow movements, where the quicker speeds help to compensate for thinner string tone and the comparative dearth of tonally alluring vibrato. Sometimes the results can sound radically different. For example, the great Adagio of Beethoven's Ninth Symphony can last any-where from eleven to more than eighteen minutes, and this in a movement which is through-composed (in other words, with no large sectional repeats). And beyond the question of pulse within a movement, there are also issues of the tempo relationships between movements, or between large sections of movements that flow at differing rates.

In all of these cases, whether in quick music or slow, the most important point to stress is that the feelings of excitement or repose, anxiety or anticipation, generated by any given tempo are as dependent on phrasing and rhythm as on actual speed. What this means in practical terms is that quick tempos can be more exciting, but they can also be stiff, mechanical, and so blurred in terms of articulation that the ear can't keep up. Very slow tempos can be seraphically tranquil, or merely flabby and dull. As with all of the other performance factors that we have been considering, each interpretation needs to be evaluated on its own merits.

The principal controversy regarding tempo in Beethoven per-formance concerns his metronome markings for individual move-ments. This handy gadget had just been developed and patented around 1816, after all of Beethoven's symphonies had been written except the Ninth, and when the composer was already totally deaf. He actually knew its inventor, Johann Mälzel, and had previously written the original version of his "battle symphony" *Wellington's Victory* for another of Mälzel's mechanical contraptions. Beethoven was of two minds about the metronome. He recognized its usefulness in fixing a tempo, but at the same time purportedly noted that "you can't put a metronome mark on sentiment."

However, the main reason that Beethoven's metronome markings are so controversial is that they are terribly fast, so much so that the music in some of the quick movements reaches the very limits of the possible. Some conductors in the early to midtwentieth century, such as Hermann Scherchen and René Liebowitz, tried to prove that Beethoven's theoretical ideal tempos were feasible. The results were mixed, with playing both thrilling and ragged in roughly equal measure. Today's musicians, both normal and HIP, can in fact play pretty cleanly at a death-defying pace given sufficient rehearsal, but this doesn't mean the results will be expressive and interesting rather than merely breathless.

By and large, all conductors and orchestras of whatever persuasion take Beethoven's metronome markings with a big grain of salt, and reserve the right to choose tempos that they believe best suit the size of the ensemble, the acoustics of the room, and the character of the music. This is exactly how it should be. There are few things in the world of classical music more tedious than an artist who takes a dogmatic view of this issue. In general, it's probably fair to say that too quick is usually better than too slow, and this can favor HIP-influenced performances in the fast movements of most symphonies. On the other hand, virtually nothing sounds less appealing than a rushed slow movement, particularly when considered within the context of the whole work, as a function of the music's contrasting moods and emotions.

Here then is the bottom line when it comes to Beethoven and the HIP movement in general: of the nine symphonies, four belong more to his Classical side (nos. 1, 2, 4, and 8), four look forward to the Romantic tradition and respond well to that style of performance (nos. 5, 6, 7 and 9), and one, the Third, is a transitional work falling squarely in the middle. Not surprisingly, the Classical works have benefited most from the HIP approach, but these are also the symphonies that listeners tend to care about the least. The bigger, more Romantic pieces have always thrived as played by today's modern orchestras. Furthermore, within the Romantic aesthetic there has always been a "classicizing" school, most tellingly represented in conducting by Toscanini and his followers (Erich and Carlos Kleiber, George Szell, Günter Wand, and many others).

In reality, Beethoven's expressive range is larger than any single school of interpretation or performance practice. The best renditions invariably do what he did: they incorporate as wide a world of feeling and technique as possible, in keeping with the demands of each symphony. If there was ever a composer whose music leaves no room for theorizing or pedantry, it's Beethoven. However, there is no doubt that the HIP movement at its best has exercised a positive influence by encouraging musicians and audiences to experience him with fresh ears. As with most new trends of this sort, its most valuable discoveries will be adopted generally— as is happening now—while the nonsense will (hopefully) fall by the wayside. Participating in this process, whether as a performer, critic, or listener, is one of the most exciting experiences in the world of classical music today.

Vocal Versus Instrumental Music

Beethoven owes much of his greatness to the fact that he was, comparatively speaking, a failure as a composer of vocal music. His faux-Haydn Mass in C was a flop. No one much cares for his oratorio *Christ on the Mount of Olives*. The composition of his single opera, *Fidelio*, was tortured and protracted, and did not encourage him to make another attempt at the genre. The *Missa Solemnis* is as notorious for its vocal impracticality as it is for its musical sublimity, while the Ninth Symphony is very much the exception that proves the rule. Its fame rests on the controversial introduction of voices into what was and largely remains a purely instrumental, abstract musical form. Indeed, the very reason that Beethoven made the attempt in the first place can be legitimately characterized as a backdoor effort to satisfy his desire to write vocal music by slipping it into a medium in which he was acknowledged supreme.

Vocal music has always been viewed, for obvious reasons, as the most truthful and direct expression of human feeling. The highest goal of instrumental performance, since the dawn of time, has been to achieve the emotional immediacy of song. In Beethoven's day, this aesthetic viewpoint was reinforced by the religious belief in man as the pinnacle of creation, and in vocal music, with or without accompanying instruments, as the vehicle most suitable for worship and prayer. In the secular world, the grandest and most elaborate form of musical entertainment was opera, whose very name, which means "works," suggests a synthesis of all of the arts then known: literature, painting, decoration, design, song, and dance.

Mozart's enduring fame throughout much of the nineteenth and early twentieth centuries rested on his reputation as the first great modern opera composer, and the primacy of vocal music also accounts for Haydn's comparative eclipse, save for his late masses and oratorios (*The Creation* and *The Seasons*). The relationship between a solo voice and the larger orchestra also lies at the foundation of the instrumental form that Mozart raised to supreme heights: the concerto. Beethoven began his career very much in this vein, but deafness and the impossibility of performing his own music derailed his career as a concerto composer just as it effectively destroyed his chances at writing another opera. Operatic vocal music, you see, had to be tailored to the needs of specific singers. To compose an opera "on spec," absent any prospect of immediate performance by a known cast, was both artistically and financially suicidal. To write a successful opera, the composer had to know who he was writing for, and this demanded, at a minimum, a functioning sense of hearing. Beethoven's late vocal works, the *Missa Solemnis* and Ninth Symphony (and the earlier *Choral*

Fantasy) are all "abstract" vocal music. The singers never assume roles as characters in a drama, as in opera, and their parts make no concessions to individual strengths or weaknesses.

The result of all of this is that Beethoven was forced, as much by circumstances as by design, to channel his energies into symphonies, quartets, piano sonatas, and works for assorted chamber ensembles. But this isn't to say that he gave up his love of the voice. Instead, he poured the most intensely vocal lyricism into his instrumental writing, creating a melodic style of unprecedented expressive power. One of the most common markings in Beethoven's scores, particularly in the late works, is *cantabile*, or "songlike." The spirit of song animates all of Beethoven's music, but particularly his slow movements, irrespective of how he actually titles them. Consider these headings from his last string quartets alone:

- Op. 127: Adagio, ma non troppo e molto cantabile [slow, but not too much and very songlike]

- Op. 131: Andante, ma non troppo e molto cantabile [same as above, except "moderately slow"]

- Op. 130: Cavatina. Adagio molto espressivo [simple song, slow and very expressive]

- Op. 132: Heiliger Dankgesang eines Genesenen an die Gottheit, in der lydischen Tonart [holy song of thanks from a convalescent to the deity, in the Lydian mode]

- Op. 135: Lento assai, cantante e tranquillo [very slow, singing and tranquil]

This is another aspect of Beethoven's enduring popularity, because throughout human history popular music has always meant "songs," and to the extent that music in larger forms stays in touch with its primal vocal roots, it has that much chance of gaining widespread acceptance and acclaim. The great irony here is that Beethoven's vocal lines are such nightmares to sing because they so often treat the voice instrumentally. His instrumental motives and melodies, on the other hand, are the most singable, or perhaps more aptly "song-imbued," of any composer's. Their vocal expressivity can be hard to describe in words, but listeners respond to it intuitively and subconsciously, experiencing Beethoven's music at a visceral level as a compelling form of direct communication.

This "singing" quality remains, to my mind, Beethoven's greatest achievement as a composer of instrumental music, one made all the more moving and heroic in that it represents his personal triumph over the crushing obstacle of deafness that fate placed in his path. Through some miraculous combination of genius, force of will, and sheer orneriness, Beethoven found countless ways to sing, in his sonatas, his string quartets, and not least, in his concertos and symphonies.

The "Nine" and Musical Progress

It is customary to divide Beethoven's musical output into three periods: early, middle, and late, sometimes attaching further descriptive names to each: youth, maturity, old age, or "the three i's"—imitation, individuality, introspection. This periodicity somewhat misleadingly omits Beethoven's actual formative years in Bonn, thus disguising the fact that the works of his first period, through about 1802 and including the first two symphonies, are hardly immature. Indeed, they established his reputation as the natural successor to Haydn and Mozart, and for many contemporary listeners unwilling to follow his later path, the early works remained his finest musical achievements precisely because they live so clearly within established tradition.

The middle period includes symphonies 3–8, although you could argue that the Third, which is clearly transitional, belongs equally with the early works, while the late period starts (according to most, but not all, scholars) with the *Hammerklavier* Piano Sonata in and around 1817. Beethoven's output had slowed considerably by this time for a number of reasons both personal and artistic. The former included health problems and ongoing battles over the custody of his nephew Karl, whom Beethoven nearly drove to kill himself with a pistol (he missed) through a toxic combination of physical possessiveness and emotional neglect.[1] More significant, however, was the increasing monumentality, complexity, and depth of works such as the Ninth Symphony, *Missa Solemnis*, *Diabelli Variations*, the five late string quartets, and the last three piano sonatas.

You might argue very convincingly that some composers have made as much or even greater progress than did Beethoven over the course of his lifetime. Haydn comes immediately to mind, particularly as he had to invent or discover much of the musical language that Beethoven took for granted. But Haydn's progress occurs over the course of 104 symphonies and 68 (and a half) string quartets, and most people, even music scholars, have little time or patience to follow such a long path from beginning to end. What makes Beethoven so special, then, is the fact that his artistic progress happens within a comparatively limited number of works, and this is particularly true of the symphonies as there are only nine of them, compared with sixteen string quartets and thirty-two piano sonatas.

Broadly speaking, composers tend to fall into two categories: those who find their style relatively early and work within it for the rest of their active lives (three excellent examples are Bach, Mendelssohn, and Tchaikovsky), and those, like Beethoven, who continue to develop stylistically as they age (including Verdi, Wagner, Stravinsky, and Mahler). The Beethovenian model suited the nineteenth century particularly well. It was a time of political and industrial revolution, and the idea of "progress" through hard work was firmly rooted in the middle-class, nineteenth-century mentality. All of this naturally benefited Beethoven's posthumous reputation as an icon of artistic integrity and independence.

---

1. As in interesting aside, Karl van Beethoven, the only son of the three Beethoven brothers (Ludwig, Carl, and Johann), survived his uncle's affections, married, and had five children, of which the only son emigrated to America and wound up working for the Michigan Central Railroad of Detroit.

In recent decades, this value system has been questioned, at least in musical terms, by the rediscovery and veneration for Bach and Mozart, as well as for other Baroque masters who wrote huge amounts of music in a very clearly delimited style (detractors say, not without some justification, that much of it "all sounds the same"). Furthermore, some of the finest twentieth-century composers belong in this latter category, including Martinu, Villa-Lobos, Poulenc, Milhaud, Prokofiev, Vaughan Williams, and Shostakovich. This does not mean that all of these composers ceased developing their musical language, but it does suggest a certain tension between finding a personal style and the sort of continual evolution that we so admire in Beethoven.

We also cannot discount the pressure coming from academia, performing arts organizations, and the recording industry, in tandem with the rise of the period instrument movement, all of whom rely to some extent on finding new "old" repertoire and selling it on the basis of the claim that it's uniformly good and valuable. Nowhere has this been more true than in the case of Mozart. It has become extremely politically incorrect in classical music circles today to assert that much of his early music is junk, despite the fact that he would have been the first to say so. This in turn offers a direct challenge to the traditional notion of how "classical music" came to be defined—as a closed book enshrining a limited number of canonical masterpieces, with Beethoven at its very center.

In one sense, the modern view seems healthy to me. There is no reason why people should not have the opportunity to hear and enjoy as much music as they please, in whatever style or manner suits them best. Loosening the definition of what constitutes a "classic" can only broaden the potential audience for so-called serious music by reducing the cultural-intimidation factor and broadening its stylistic range. The unfortunate side effect of this potential boon to consumers, however, is a somewhat specious and self-serving egalitarianism on the part of the classical music industry, insinuating that just because something is old, it must be a "classic" in the traditional, canonical sense, and that everything is just as wonderful as everything else.

The best way to counter this argument is to listen to any Beethoven symphony, for there can be no denying the reality of his supreme achievement evidenced by his progress from the early masterpieces to the late. The attitude toward the classics that prevails today has many positive elements, but these should not be allowed to diminish our ability, or undermine our right, to discriminate in a positive sense, to devote the limited leisure time that we have for listening to the best and most rewarding pieces. In this respect, Beethoven's symphonies seem likely to maintain their centrality, with their undeniable quality and dynamic stylistic trajectory acting as a bulwark against the less savory aspects of cultural relativism.

Cultural Economics and the Rise of the Beethoven Industry

Economists will tell you that there's value in scarcity, and this is as true of the arts as it is of any other commodity. The fact that Beethoven wrote only nine symphonies has contributed tremendously to our ability to perceive their value. Mozart's reputation as a symphonist is sustained by the fact that we treasure his last six works in this form and (until recently at least) conveniently ignored the rest. Haydn's role as "the father of the symphony" hasn't stopped succeeding generations from reducing his output to a mere handful of popular pieces despite the fact that dozens of symphonies are just as marvelous, and none can be considered immature (he didn't start writing them until he was in his late twenties).

Indeed, the magic number nine has become so potent a symbol that few symphonic composers managed to remain unaffected by it. Some, like Dvořák and Vaughan Williams, actually wrote just nine symphonies, although Dvořák went to his grave believing that his first had been irretrievably lost. Others who wrote more than that (Bruckner and Mahler, for example) nevertheless wound up with nine formally *numbered* works. Schubert's symphonies also traditionally number nine even though there is no seventh, and he left a whole bunch of incomplete fragments in addition to the famous "Unfinished" Symphony. Sibelius also wrote nine symphonies, declining to assign numbers to *Kullervo* and the four-movement *Lemminkäinen* Suite, while still including them in the total count from the safe vantage point of his lengthy retirement. Swedish composer Kurt Atterberg's Ninth and final symphony even includes vocal parts, in direct homage to Beethoven.

Some composers who went beyond the quasi-biblical number nine, such as George Lloyd and Dmitri Shostakovich, deliberately made their respective Ninth Symphonies light and pithy, in the latter case much to the displeasure of the Soviet authorities who insisted that Beethoven's model *had* to be redefined in socialist realist terms—or else. But however many symphonies a composer ultimately wrote after Beethoven, it has always been assumed that the seriousness and "bigness" of the form militates against the kind of fecundity typical of earlier times. Composers who wrote lots of symphonies, such as Havergal Brian or Nikolai Myaskovsky, have had a hard time finding an audience even for their best works. Being tarred as "uneven" is a serious artistic offense.

This is because the most precious of all intangible commodities is trust, the belief that a large work, difficult to rehearse and costly to produce, is worth both the player's and the listener's time and effort. It was true in Beethoven's day, and it's just as true in ours. Nevertheless, Beethoven obviously was not laboring under the weight of subsequent history, and given the personal factors—such as his increasing deafness—that encouraged him to continue as a symphonist, we may do well to ask why he wrote so few. The traditional argument holds that his music's increasing length and complexity precluded the kind of mass production that Mozart and Haydn managed, but this is only correct to a degree. The five late string quartets are just as imposing as, and certainly no less intricate than, the Ninth Symphony. There were other external forces in play as well.

The most significant of these was war—specifically, the Napoleonic Wars. The first decade of the nineteenth century saw the fall of Vienna, and not only did this disrupt concert life, there were the economic hardships occasioned by the need to raise, supply, and direct the Austrian army. Under these circumstances, the aristocracy, whose principal job, let us not forget, was to defend the country, had other things to do than live a life of leisure and patronize the arts. Private orchestras, theaters, and opera houses such as those Haydn's patron supported, are expensive enough in peacetime, never mind war and economic depression. Of course, musical life goes on, particularly in a city like Vienna, even under foreign occupation, but it just so happens that Beethoven's "middle period" coincides exactly with the height of the war.

It's remarkable, then, that he wrote as many symphonies during this time as he did. Another effect of social unrest is to reduce or eliminate the possibility of writing works to commission, particularly foreign ones. The Ninth Symphony, for example, was created at the behest of the Philharmonic Society of London. Had Beethoven not been deaf, if he had been able to lead the life of a traveling virtuoso as did Mozart in his childhood or even Haydn at the end of his life, or assume the directorship of a full-time arts institution as Liszt did in Weimar or Spohr in Kassel, he might have had more reason to compose specific works for his tours, his various patrons, or his own ensemble. As it was, he was forced to live the life of a recluse and subsist for the most part on the largess of the Viennese aristocracy.

These are some of the reasons, then, that account for the relative scarcity of Beethoven symphonies, and consequently some of their heightened value as individual works. But even the laws of cultural economics could not have anticipated our modern world, in which literally thousands of orchestras play these same nine pieces constantly, and music lovers have the luxury of choosing from among countless recordings dating all the way back to Arthur Nikisch's famous 1913 acoustic recording of the Fifth Symphony with the Berlin Philharmonic. Happily, overproduction doesn't diminish the absolute cultural worth of a work of art, only the price people are willing to pay to experience it live or purchase a copy for home consumption.

In Beethoven's time music lovers familiarized themselves with the symphonies by playing piano transcriptions tailored to keyboard amateurs, some of whom, particularly among the women, were in fact every bit as good as professionals. At a more technically challenging level, there are also the famous arrangements of all nine symphonies made by Liszt. These have been recorded multiple times, and are well worth hearing for the light they shed on musical texture, particularly Beethoven's bass lines, which emerge with far more clarity played by the left hand than they typically do in the orchestra where high-pitched instruments dominate. Music publishers at this time made their living by serving this play-at-home market. This was the first Beethoven industry.

With the rise of full-time professional orchestras, not to mention record companies, sheet music publishers found themselves on the horns of a dilemma. On the one hand, they were committed to publishing reams of modern music that, particularly in the twentieth century, no one cared much about or wanted to play. The domestic market had long since dried up as radio and recordings made it unnecessary to learn instruments and play the classics at home. By the same token, the most popular works at symphony concerts were Classical and Romantic standards by long-dead composers, most if not all of which either were not protected by copyright (and had never been), or were soon entering the public domain.

One admittedly partial solution has taken the form of the "critical edition." Periodically some musical scholar, at the urging of a prominent publisher, will return to the manuscript sources and prepare a new, theoretically scholarly text that supposedly captures the composer's original intentions according to the latest research and methodology. Often this means removing the editorial editions and amendments of prior publishers, or deciding tiny points of detail based on multiple sources (draft sketches, copyist scores, first editions with composer's corrections, and suchlike). Publish the result and—Voila!—Bach, Haydn, Mozart, and Beethoven are now back in copyright, at least if performers want to claim to be *au courant*. This practice has become the second Beethoven industry.

Not surprisingly, the critical edition and "urtext" (German for "original text") mania currently sweeping the classical music universe finds itself closely aligned with the period instrument movement. The necessity for such editions, financial considerations aside, varies widely from composer to composer. It has been absolutely necessary in the case of Haydn, not only because many previously unpublished works have appeared in print for the first time, but also because the printed scores and parts in general circulation of his most frequently played symphonies, at least until a few decades ago, were notably corrupt and unreliable. So I don't mean to raise a cynical eyebrow at work that serves this sort of musically meaningful purpose.

The issue with Beethoven's symphonies is more complicated, if only because they have been played continuously since they were first composed, and have thus been subject to more scrutiny as regards the basic text than virtually any other music in the standard repertoire. There are exactly two possibly meaningful issues that recent critical editions have attempted to solve. The first concerns repeats in the scherzo (third movement) of the Fifth Symphony; Beethoven originally planned to have the basic ABA structure repeated: ABABA, as in the Fourth, Sixth, and Seventh Symphonies. Later he canceled the repeat for reasons we will discuss in considering the symphony in the next chapter. The new C. F. Peters edition restores this repeat, and you can hear it in Kurt Masur's not terribly exciting second Beethoven cycle with the Leipzig Gewandhaus Orchestra on Philips. Jonathan del Mar's Bärenreiter edition, on the other hand, removes the repeat once again. Del Mar's seems to be on its way to becoming the standard modern text; at least it has been the one most widely adopted in recent recordings.

The other issue concerns the dynamics of the eruptive timpani solos in the scherzo of the Ninth Symphony. Traditionally, the last of them has been played softly and mysteriously, but Del Mar finds no support for this interpretation. John Eliot Gardiner in his period instrument cycle claimed that they should be performed in a steady diminuendo, but this view hasn't been widely adopted and, more the point, tends to sound fussy.

In your wanderings through the thickets of live and recorded Beethoven, whether on period or modern instruments, you are thus quite likely to encounter claims regarding the importance of the edition being used. Ignore them. They are meaningless. Of course it's nice to start with the composer's original text, and far be it from me to deny publishers the right to make a living renting out the only music that audiences really want to hear and orchestras are likely to play. But the fact is that normal differences from one interpretation to the next are far more likely to outweigh the tiny minutiae concerning placement of accents, slurs, ties, minor adjustments in dynamics, and other insignificant points of musical punctuation that serve to justify the latest Beethoven critical editions.

Indeed, even if you could truly hear the distinctions between texts, there is absolutely no guarantee that the performers will actually *play* the music that way on the night of the performance. So don't worry about it. Just rest assured that all Beethoven editions are basically the same in the way that matters most: they give the performers the information necessary to deliver a thrilling performance more or less in keeping with the composer's original intentions. Remember that the printed score is not the piece itself; it is the recipe for a sonic experience that creates itself anew, moving through time, whenever it's played. As the great Talmudic sage Hillel once noted, "All the rest is commentary."

Chapter 2

Symphony no. 5 in C Minor, Op. 67 (1808)

1. Allegro con brio (quickly, with verve)
2. Andante con moto (walking tempo, with movement)
3. Scherzo: Allegro [leading without pause into . . .]
4. Finale: Allegro

Orchestration: piccolo, 2 flutes, 2 oboes, 2 clarinets, 2 bassoons, contrabassoon, 2 trumpets, 2 horns, 3 trombones, strings

Program of the premiere at Beethoven's Akademie of December 22, 1808:

PART 1
Symphony No. 6 "Pastoral" [Originally billed as No. 5]
Concert Aria: "Ah, Perfido" [Josephine Killitschgy, soprano]
"Hymn" with Latin Text [From Mass in C major]
Piano Concerto No. 4 [Beethoven at the piano]

PART 2
Symphony No. 5 [Originally billed as No. 6]
"Sanctus" with Latin Text [From Mass in C major]
Fantasia for Solo Piano [Beethoven at the piano]
Choral Fantasy [Beethoven at the piano]

THE FIFTH SYMPHONY had its first performance on the above program, in which every number was advertised as a public premiere. For some odd reason, this concert is often described as containing upwards of four hours of music. I have no doubt that it may have lasted that long, what with the need to rearrange the orchestra, set up the chorus, and leave time between numbers (including an intermission between the two halves). Nevertheless, the actual musical duration could not have been more than about two and a half hours. This was surely more than enough considering the fact that all of the pieces were unfamiliar, difficult to execute, and modern in style.

An *Akademie* is essentially a benefit event. Beethoven was responsible for hiring the performers, renting the hall, printing and selling tickets, and advertising the event. In exchange, he kept all of the profits (if any) after expenses. The concert of December 22 was famously disastrous. The orchestra was underrehearsed and alienated. Beethoven had already antagonized his soprano of choice, and her replacement was so terrified that he had to drag her onstage to flub her way through her aria. The hall was unheated, the event poorly attended, and God only knows how the music must have sounded. From contemporary reports, the words "noisy and chaotic" perhaps sum it up best.

The Fifth Symphony was by no means the popular success that it later became. This is not surprising; most new and complex works take time to sink in and establish themselves, but the reaction of Beethoven's contemporary Louis Spohr is instructive. In his autobiography, Spohr writes about a performance of the piece that he heard in Munich in 1815:

> Though with many individual beauties, yet it does not consti-
> tute a classical whole. For instance, the introductory theme of
> the very first passage is wanting in that dignity which according
> to my feeling the commencement of a Symphony should of a
> necessity possess. Setting this aside, the short and easily com-
> prehended theme, certainly permits of being carried out very

thematically, and is combined also by the composer with the other principal ideas of the first subject in an ingenious and effective manner. The Adagio in A-flat is in part very fine, yet the same passages and modulations repeat themselves much too frequently, and although always with richer ornamentation, become in the end wearisome. The Scherzo is highly original, and of real romantic coloring, but the Trio with the noisy running bass is to my taste much too rough. The concluding passage with its unmeaning noise, is the least satisfactory; nevertheless the return to the Scherzo at this part is so happy an idea, that the composer may be envied for it. Its effect is most captivating! But what a pity that this impression is so soon obliterated by the returning noise!

Spohr, who greatly admired Beethoven's early music and performed it regularly, put his finger on exactly those "popular" elements that characterize the works of his middle period: the outwardly simple but obstinately memorable themes, directness of expression amounting to roughness, noisy climaxes, and faith in Classical harmony. Many later composers, Spohr in particular, regarded musical progress almost entirely in harmonic terms. Their love of continual modulation (movement between keys), as their own works sometimes show, undermines the more highly organized treatment of tonality that gives Beethoven's sonata movements their motive force and feeling of goal-directed energy.

Yet Spohr was also forced to acknowledge Beethoven's developmental and formal brilliance, and it is of course the combination of supreme compositional craft applied to material seemingly of great simplicity, along with the willingness to "let it all hang out" at the climaxes, that we now recognize as characteristically Beethovenian. There is in all of the music of his middle period a certain rabble-rousing quality that cultural snobs (of which the classical music world has more than its fair share) have always found offensive, and this quality is nowhere more evident than in precisely those parts of the Fifth Symphony to which Spohr most strenuously objected. Indeed, this quality has made the Fifth the most famous symphony in history, the one that everyone, whether they like classical music or not, immediately recognizes.

ORCHESTRATION AND SOUND WORLD

Many composers differentiate and characterize specific works through their handling of the orchestra, and this is also true of the Fifth Symphony. Its basic sonority is deliberately massive. Hearing it often produces the feeling that the full orchestra has been playing much of the time. Solo or lightly textured episodes aren't unusual, but they exist to offer contrast to the more heavily scored *tuttis* (passages for the full ensemble). For the first time in a symphony that anyone cares about, we find parts for piccolo, three trombones, and contrabassoon, albeit in the finale only. Note the proportions: one bright, high-pitched instrument to four dark, low ones.

The issue of the use of the contrabassoon has been discussed by, among others, Charles Mackerras, who notes that the instrument appears only in the finale, and has no independent part (it plays along with the basses). Mackerras points out quite reasonably that it makes no sense at all to have a separate player sit around for three movements doing nothing, and that in Beethoven's day the contrabassoonist, unless he doubled on some other instrument the rest of the time, quite likely took part in the rest of the symphony as well. This makes sense, particularly as you will probably never hear a note of the contrabassoon in any case (or at least you should not, as that instrument's gruff timbre merges perfectly with that of the strings). So don't be surprised if in concert you see what looks like a large piece of mahogany-colored plumbing puffing its way through this or any symphony without making any significant aural impression. A couple of pictorial blasts in Haydn's *The Creation* aside, until we get to Mahler in the late nineteenth century, this is what contrabassoons usually do.

The piccolo and trombones, on the other hand, really do give the finale added brilliance on the one hand, and festive solemnity on the other. In keeping with the symphony's unusually weighty atmosphere, Beethoven also gives extra prominence to the bassoons and the lower strings. The former have notable solo licks in the first movement (controversially, as we will see), andante, and scherzo, while the latter lead off both the second and third movements, and make the scherzo's central "trio" section the most famous *tour de force* for a bass section in all of symphonic literature. The two French horns also make very important contributions in the last two movements, so much so that that it's not unusual to see the parts doubled.

The finale, by virtue of having the trombones, naturally makes a big show of the brass section, and Beethoven's restraint in saving them for the finale became standard practice in the Romantic period among composers of a more conservative bent. Two famous examples include the First and Fourth Symphonies of Brahms, both of which reserve the trombones for the finale, where they lend the music additional weight and power, exactly as they do in Beethoven's Fifth. Even Berlioz, in his *Symphonie Fantastique* (1830)—that musical calling card of the Romantic period— waited until his fourth movement (of five) before cutting loose the trombones.

These are all very general observations, but they are worth keeping in mind as you listen to any highly organized piece of orchestral music because timbre often functions not just as distinctive color, but also as a unifying principle, relating the work's various parts to each other and contributing to the impression that the individual movements really stand together to form the complex of emotional expression that makes up the larger whole. Traditional musical analysis does a very poor job of giving these easily audible devices their due, preferring instead to emphasize direct thematic recall or strict development and variation, but as you will see in the discussion of both symphonies, Beethoven works very hard to give each what Verdi would call its *tinta*, or "color." We will refer to this fact quite often in the movement-by-movement discussion that follows.

FIRST MOVEMENT

This first movement offers a textbook example of what later came to be known as "sonata form." There are two contrasting themes, or "subjects," one tense and agitated in the home key of C minor, the other calmly lyrical in a contrasting major mode. These comprise the "exposition." The ensuing "development" section is one of Beethoven's most compact, and the argument is extremely easy to follow. It leads to a very regular "recapitulation," in which the two principal subjects return in the same order, culminating in a tremendously exciting coda that functions almost like a second development section, and which has the purpose of reasserting the angry minor key in which the movement began.

This bare-bones description, while accurate as far as it goes, obviously says nothing about what makes the music so expressively powerful, nor does it hint at those elements of Beethoven's personal style that make his approach to sonata form unlike anyone else's. In fact, the music's formal simplicity and compression constitutes one of its most radical and astonishing qualities. Recall that in the previous chapter I suggested that works in sonata form contrast two basic kinds of material: thematic "subjects," which may include any number of tunes and motives, and transitional ideas or "motion music." Subjects live within a particular key, which they clearly define, while the transitional material often lacks obvious melodic interest, offering instead a correspondingly higher level of activity, conveying a sense of "going somewhere."

In the Fifth Symphony, Beethoven effectively blurs the distinction between these two kinds of music right where it matters most—in the transition between the first and second subjects. In other words, the first subject has the energy of motion music, while the motion music, until the big blast of sound at its very end, has just as much thematic interest as a typical first subject. Beethoven accomplishes this by the simple expedient of building the motion music so relentlessly out of the four-note opening motive that it's impossible to draw a firm line between it and the first subject proper.

The result, formally speaking, is an exposition that encompasses two big, highly differentiated musical paragraphs, each composed of exactly two sentences. Despite the typical descriptions of this movement, which often emphasize the brevity of the symphony's opening motto and the mosaic-like character of the tunes derived from it, the music is actually much more noteworthy for its continuity, for the length and breadth of its phrases. Noted musicologist, conductor, and program-note writer Donald Francis Tovey pointed this very fact out at the beginning of the last century, and rightly so. What Beethoven has achieved is genuine bigness of utterance packed into an unusually compact space, a quality that gives the movement so much of its tension and explosive energy.

Beethoven didn't discover this technique. You can find something very similar in many of Haydn's later symphonies; if you have time, check out the finale of Symphony no. 86 for a particularly telling example of a very similar procedure. In fact, there is a famous string quartet by Haydn (Op. 50, no. 4 in F-sharp minor) whose first movement uses a four-note motive very similar to the one that opens this symphony almost as obsessively as does Beethoven. But then, Beethoven himself also exploits it to totally different expressive effect in his Fourth Piano Concerto.

Nevertheless, if Beethoven can't be said to have invented the concept of making whole sections of his sonata-form expositions thematic, he certainly reinvented it, and made the technique his own. You can hear him working toward this goal starting with the first movement of the Third Symphony, getting closer in the Fourth, and finally arriving at his ideal in the opening movements of the Fifth and Sixth Symphonies. Nevertheless, please don't get the impression that formal gambits such as this, particularly in Beethoven, arise from the application of some sort of abstract theoretical concept. On the contrary, they evolve naturally from the nature and design of the themes themselves. Beethoven spent a considerable part of his compositional time hammering his various subjects into a shape that is perfectly suited to both their formal and expressive treatment.

The famous four-note motto, twice repeated, that opens the symphony presents conductors with one of their most notorious interpretive challenges. Achieving the degree of vehemence that Beethoven evidently demands while maintaining good ensemble isn't easy, even given the generally excellent technical quality of modern orchestras. Scored only for strings and clarinets, the question immediately arises: Why such a comparatively light scoring for such a powerful opening? The answer, in hindsight, is that Beethoven wanted to keep something in reserve for the extremely powerful climaxes later on. Just why he felt that the clarinets were necessary remains a mystery. You certainly won't hear them, and in those extremely rare instances where you can, just barely, as in some of the more radically wrongheaded period instrument performances, it's only because there aren't enough strings to give the music its proper weight and force.

Aside from keeping the opening together rhythmically (even a renowned Beethoven conductor such as Wilhelm Furtwängler seldom managed it), the biggest interpretive issue is one of timing. Is this an introduction or not? Beethoven has placed fermatas, or "hold" signs over the motive's final, long note, and has added an additional half note to its second iteration. This means, in most performances, that the latter should be held slightly longer than the former. But how long should that be?

Giving the fermatas a generous amount of time tends to detach this opening from the rest of the movement, creating an imposing introduction, but at the cost of some energy and momentum that Beethoven surely intended to be present from the beginning. It's a problem that has no single solution, and it depends very much on the larger context—particularly on the tempo relationships between this opening and the main body of the movement. This is just one of the many reasons that the music never sounds quite the same twice and exercises such a continuing fascination—and we're still only discussing the first few measures.

Now let's look at the first subject a bit more closely. As just noted, it consists of two musical sentences. Each begins with the four-note "fate" motive, or motto. Beethoven scores the first sentence for strings alone, with just a little help from the bassoons until the full orchestra (minus the piccolo, contrabassoon, and trombones until the finale) joins in at the very end. The second sentence starts with the horns and woodwinds joining the strings in a louder version of the opening motive, and then works its way with full ensemble participation in a swiftly gathering crescendo to a loud, dissonant climax that cuts off abruptly.

All of this music is based on ceaseless repetition of the symphony's motto, but the important thing to notice is that the second sentence is much longer than the first. In other words, the music wants to expand, to get bigger and more intense. This makes the cutoff all the more surprising when it happens, and it helps to produce tension, a feeling of potential that remains as yet unfulfilled. In short, the music needs to continue, and although this is one of those feelings that can't really be described in words, you sense it immediately while listening.

Beethoven's treatment of harmony at the end of this first subject, combined with his other methods of driving the music forward, creates the definite impression of "arrival and continuing" as the second subject chimes in with a bell-like variant of the motto on the two French horns. Remember this particular motive. Not only will it serve as the most important and fascinating object of development in the whole movement, it also reveals a fact that more pedantic views of sonata form often ignore: the music has in fact been "developing" right from the very first bar. This was another technique that Beethoven learned from Haydn, one that he will apply in even more extreme (and Haydnesque) form in the first movement of the Seventh Symphony.

If the first subject was anxious and full of angry gestures and outbursts, the second is just the opposite: calm, lyrical, major-key, and smoothly articulated in equal notes—as least as far as its first sentence. This takes the form of a quiet dialogue between the first violins, then clarinet, then violins with flute, softly accompanied by the bassoons, second violins, and violas, additionally underpinned by mutterings of the motto by the cellos and basses. Beethoven starts to build tension once again immediately in the simplest possible way: by cutting the phrase lengths in half, from their initial eight notes to four, and repeating the resulting motive over and over in a mounting crescendo.

At the top of the crescendo, the orchestra gives a *tutti* shout which spills over into the next sentence in quicker tempo (actually, the overall speed remains the same but the note values are shorter), still based on repetitions of that tiny four-note motive in the violins, sharply punctuated by accented chords from the rest of the orchestra, including the trumpets and timpani. With masterly inevitability, this second subject's four-note motive morphs into the symphony's opening motto, filtering down twice through the wind section, bringing the exposition to its close very decisively in a mood close to triumph.

There are two major points that stand out here. The first is that, like the previous subject, the second's pair of sentences undergo a process of intensification, from slow, soft, and lyrical to quick, loud, rhythmic, and joyous. Indeed, the contrast between the two sentences is even greater in this case, so much so that the major-key mood of the second subject colors the symphony's opening motto, giving it a still vigorous but essentially amiable character. The exposition repeat, if taken (and it should be), thus drives home with particular force the emotional distance between the start of the symphony and the end of the exposition.

This is where the analogy between sonata form as a linear journey tends to break down. A staged drama or story seldom has time to go back to the beginning and start over. But as this exposition only lasts a couple of minutes, and perception of the events to come depends to some extent on your memory of the various characters initially presented, Beethoven and his contemporaries can afford to indulge in sectional repetition. In later Romantic and modern music, where "expositions" are often lengthened considerably, the value in making a repeat becomes much less obvious and composers generally either accepted the fact that they were

optional (as did Brahms), or wrote in conscious imitation of classical models and so expected similar rules to apply (for example,
Shostakovich's Ninth Symphony).

It's also worth noting in this connection that Beethoven has
crafted the ending of the exposition to create a bit of "What will
happen next?" suspense by extending it for two and a half bars of
notated silence beyond the last note sounded. He does the same
thing, albeit less effectively, in the first movement of the Seventh
Symphony (but not in the Sixth), and the creative use of rests,
or silence, is almost always an indication that the composer is
thinking in terms of the effect the repeat will have on the listener,
and not merely obeying blindly some convention or rule of form.
And of course, having heard the exposition again and come to the
same expectant silence, the start of the next section becomes all
the more impressive.

The development begins, like every major part of the movement, with the opening motto, here blasted out by the horns and
clarinets, and followed by the strings, but in a harmonic position
that seems more curious or questioning than sternly declamatory.
The first subject enters quietly on the violins, veering off in gentle
dialogue between strings and woodwind into several different keys
before starting one of Beethoven's by now famous crescendos by
motivic repetition, in this case of the opening motto. At the climax, the orchestra reaches a paroxysm of fury interspersed by brief
silences—a fit of shouting punctuated by pauses for breath so as to
resume yelling even louder.

Next comes one of the most famous passages in all of
Beethoven. He "deconstructs" the six-note horn call that began
the second subject in a way that's truly marvelous. First, let me
draw your attention to a detail that's often overlooked. The process
of deconstruction actually begins at the previous climax, when the
four-note motto emerges reduced only to three. This new version
works its way in sequence through the woodwind section from the
bottom up, above repetitions in the strings of the second subject's
horn call. These wind parts are extremely difficult to hear clearly if

the strings don't make a strong diminuendo to get out of their way (Otto Klemperer's stereo EMI recording with the Philharmonia Orchestra is unsurpassed here), which is contrary to Beethoven's actual notation. It's an interpretive problem with no obvious solution, though I personally lean toward adjusting the dynamics to make the texture as clear as possible.

Only after two repetitions of the above process does Beethoven then apply the same principal of deconstruction to the six-note horn call, reducing it in dialogue between strings and winds to a mere two notes, then only one chiming chord alternating between the sections. This passage reveals with incredible power and concision the ability of the sonata style to control the listener's subjective perception of movement. Time seems suspended, even though an angry interruption of the full horn call reminds us that the actual tempo remains virtually unchanged. At this point, then, the music appears to be stuck, repeating a gently dissonant, amorphous chord over and over. Suddenly the "fate" motto echoes through the orchestra, and in just a couple of seconds the recapitulation arrives, emphasized this time by the full ensemble with trumpets and timpani.

This development section has been remarkable in several ways. It's very short, and like the first and second subjects it consists of two large sentences. The word "development," however, is misleading in this connection, at least to the extent that it suggests a sort of steady progress, a "building up" or "working through" (a literal translation of the German term for development, *Durchführung*) of the previously heard material. Here, the first subject appears only briefly, and the main body of the second subject not even once. The most important building block, the transitional horn call that introduces the second subject, doesn't evolve at all. Quite the opposite: it simply disintegrates, making the arrival of the recapitulation not the inevitable outcome of a serenely logical process but rather a violent interruption arising out of frustration.

In other words, the process of the music might very well be described as *irrational*, as expressions of rage so often are.

Beethoven's handling of form remains pellucidly clear, even as the emotional expression articulated by that form breaks all bounds of decorum in its directness and truthfulness. Even so, the first subject, when it returns, finds itself changed by its brief sojourn though the development section. Alongside the anxiously chattering violins, a lyrical countermelody takes shape in the bassoons, gets handed off to the oboe, and continues beyond the end of the first sentence as a brief, mournful, and inimitably moving solo that gives the entire orchestra a moment to pause for reflection.

This brief moment of intimacy makes the continuation of the first subject (its second sentence) all the more powerful, and you can hear very clearly the difference in harmony this time around at the sharp closing chord that allows Beethoven to keep the second subject in the major versions of his the home key. This is further confirmed when the six-note, transitional motive now appears on the bassoons, with the horns contributing only to its last note. For most of the Romantic period performers and scholars gave this motive back to the horns as in the exposition, arguing that Beethoven would have used them but for the fact that the natural (valveless) horns in his day simply didn't have time to retune (they actually had replaceable bits of piping, or "crooks," for this purpose).

There is no question that the motive sounds as if Beethoven imagined it specifically for the timbre of the horns, or that it has a tendency to sound comical when given to the bassoons. At the same time, we can't dismiss the possibility that the use of woodwinds here continues that "softening" process inaugurated by the lyrical oboe solo, or that Beethoven consciously wished to avoid literal repetition. Given the importance of the bassoons throughout the symphony, this is another one of those interpretive issues that has no definitive solution. It hardly violates Beethoven's conception to have the horns play here, but by the same token there is no reason that the bassoons need to make the motive sound silly.

Beethoven rescores the second subject to sound even more ethereal than previously, now as a dialogue between first violins and flute (later doubled by a clarinet). The same climax built from four-note half-phrases leads to the joyful second sentence, and the final cadence that brings back the friendly version of the motto. Instead of reaching a complete stop, however, the full orchestra with trumpets well to the fore wrenches the harmony back to tense minor keys and races forward angrily. This passage, built entirely of the "fate" motto, might be rendered in dialogue as follows:

Orchestra (loudly enraged): Stand back, I'm coming through!

Horns, bassoons, and clarinets (quietly and timidly): Are you sure?

Orchestra (even more angrily): Damn right. Out of my way!

Full woodwinds, trumpets and timpani (strongly): Yes, sir!

In other words, in just a few seconds of musical dialogue Beethoven gives the motto several distinctly different emotional colorations. Imagine a scene in which the script contained nothing but a single repeated word, but the actors had to convey a full range of meanings and still tell the story entirely through variations in vocal timbre and volume. This is one of the things that music, aided by harmony and tone color, does particularly well, and it's a skill that Beethoven cultivates in this movement to a hitherto unimaginable degree of sophistication. But that's not the best part of this coda.

After the above exchange, Beethoven picks up where the development section left off, starting with the six-note transitional motive, atop which the violins make threatening gestures. These finally descend through the orchestra in a graphic representation of turmoil made all the more powerful by being basically athematic. In other words, its two principal components are loudness and busyness, and when melody returns in the form of a brutal dialogue between the winds and strings, Beethoven works the most wonderful thematic transformation in the entire symphony (and as you will hear, there are others).

The four-note expletives that make up this passage all derive directly from the lyrical second subject's half-phrases. Their emotional character is so different that you may miss the relationship entirely, but once you know where to look it becomes quite evident.

Here again, Beethoven shows how form and content work hand in hand to create extraordinary expressive intensity. Formally, this coda actually continues and completes the development section by working with material that was ignored previously. Emotionally, by turning what was once a sweetly placid melody into a vicious duel between orchestral sections in the movement's turbulent minor (home) tonality, Beethoven creates a gripping musical narrative in which rage and violence triumph over peace and tranquility.

Having won the second subject over to the "dark side," Beethoven can bring the movement home as it began, with the opening fate motto, now blazingly victorious (in an evil sense) and blasted out by the full orchestra. It should be clear at this point why Beethoven opened the symphony with the same music scored only for strings and clarinets; he was saving his heavy artillery for just this point. After a few timid, pathetic gestures from the strings and woodwinds that serve only to confirm fate's complete dominance, the movement thunders to a close with abrupt finality.

This description of the movement's emotional climate has been very conservative as far as the Beethoven literature goes. The feelings that the music arouses and the story that it tells naturally vary from person to person, and from writer to writer. In the nineteenth century, for example, Sir George Grove (of Grove's Dictionary of Music and Musicians fame) proposed the idea that the first and second subjects represented, respectively, Beethoven himself and his one-time fiancée, Countess Theresa Brunswick, with the music charting the course of their failed relationship. Unless the countess turned very nasty at the end, this strikes me as unlikely, but Grove's view is very typical of the Romantic view of Beethoven's music, as well as the tendency to seek clarification of the music's meaning in the composer's biography.

The real point is that everyone agrees that the first movement of the Fifth Symphony expresses the idea of "conflict." For a wonderful visual realization of this notion, turn to the classic 1950s television sketch "Argument to Beethoven's Fifth." Featuring Sid Caesar and Nanette Fabray, the sketch features the two miming a domestic dispute to the entire first movement, significantly minus the exposition repeat, with wonderful visual specificity. You can find it on DVD in the first volume of *The Sid Caesar Collection*, and, crazy as it may sound, it really does portray in real time the ebb and flow of the Beethoven's musical narrative better than any other source, literary or otherwise, than I have ever encountered. Besides, it's hilarious, the joke arising from the very fact that the story being told is so true to the music itself.

SECOND MOVEMENT

This lovely *Andante con moto* (walking pace, with movement) forms as great a contrast as possible to the first movement while still managing to capture ideas that we will come to recognize as characteristic of the symphony as a whole. It takes the form of a theme with three simple variations and a substantial coda. The principal element that it shares with the other parts of the symphony, one which will become more prominent as the work proceeds, is that of a triumphant march. This forms a natural antithesis to the first movement's evocation of conflict. It is represented by a theme that begins gracefully on violas and cellos, but ends as a grand procession for trumpets, horns, and timpani.

The character of this theme appears all the more remarkable when you consider that the meter of this movement, 3/8, is one of the lightest in all music, one often reserved for lilting dances or melodies of a folklike cast. By writing against the metrical grain, as it were, Beethoven creates tension and gets the lift, the *moto* that the music must have, and also has the advantage of a strong rhythmic contrast with the first movement. Maximizing variety is always important in large works such as symphonies and sonatas, because no matter how attractive the scoring or memorable the melodies, too much rhythmic sameness will always make the music sound rigid and flat over the long haul.

Theme-and-variations form always tends to break up the music into discreet chunks, and so this andante inevitably lacks the drama of the first movement. If sonata form is dramatic, then variation form is rhetorical—a series of increasingly elaborate statements that amplify a single idea. The theme is quite long and highly varied, so the movement comes across as satisfyingly spacious without becoming excessively repetitious. Spohr's complaint about the music's repetitiveness no doubt stems from the fact that Beethoven's variations seldom stray far from the theme, which is of course exactly what gives the music its simple dignity and optimism.

The main theme has the form ABB. Its initial "A" section is that graceful tune for violas and cellos previously mentioned. Pay particular attention to the rhythm of its continuation, that alternation of long and sort notes: dum, dadum, dadum, etc. This is called a "dotted rhythm" because of the way it's often notated. Beethoven has something special in store for it that you'll see later. "B" is the march, and its phrases begin with a foreshortened version of the same rhythm: dum, dadum (after a lovely transition exchanged between strings and winds also based on this rhythm). First played softly on the clarinets and bassoons, a brief moment of hesitation leads to the march bursting out anew in the oboes, horns, trumpets, cellos, basses, and timpani, accompanied by rolling triplets (three notes squeezed into the space of two) in the rest of the strings.

This grand version of the march evaporates into gentle queries from the violins in the dotted rhythm, and a smooth transition for stings leads us back to the beginning, or in this case the first variation. This turns the melody of "A," still on violas and cellos, into a flowing stream of calm sixteenth notes, followed by an almost exact repetition of the two statements of the march—almost, because its accompaniment speeds up from triplets to straight thirty-second notes (that is, four notes instead of three in the same amount of time). This subtle touch gently increases the feeling of forward movement and prevents the repetition from sounding merely mechanical. It is utterly typical of Beethoven's precise attention to detail.

In between the two statements of the march, as well as immediately in the transition to the next variation, you may note a very rhythmic figure in the cellos. Some commentators hear a faint echo of the symphony's fate motto at this point, while others call it mere coincidence, noting that the actual figure itself has six notes rather than four. There's no definitive answer, but I tend toward the latter view for two reasons: First, the very concept of binding all the movements of a symphony together with recurring themes belongs to the later, Romantic period (starting with Berlioz's *Symphonie fantastique*). Second, if we really accept that Beethoven meant his motto to symbolize fate, then its timid, emotionally ambivalent quasi-appearance here can only confuse the issue. Fate does return, as it turns out, in the scherzo. At that point there's little question about what Beethoven intended, and the presence of the motto there, back in the home key of C minor, is much more in keeping with the character and expressive climate of the first movement, which makes good logical sense. We will encounter another musically similar situation with a very different expressive meaning in the finale.

The second variation continues the trend of acceleration by writing in ever smaller note values. Instead of flowing sixteenth notes, the entire first part of the theme appears in rapid thirty-second notes, first quietly on the violins with lovely flecks of color from the woodwinds, then steamrolling through the cellos and basses *forte*, below a chugging accompaniment from the rest of the orchestra. It's one of those moments where you really need to hear the bass line if the melody isn't to come out as a sort of dull, blurry rumble in the depths of the orchestra.

Period instrument performances, with their very fast tempos and weak bass sections, often do poorly (witness John Eliot Gardiner on Archiv), but even the highly regarded Carlos Kleiber recording with the bottom-heavy Vienna Philharmonic (DG) is far from ideal. Four conductors who deliver the goods in the passage are Dorati (Mercury Living Presence), Szell (Sony), Vänskä (BIS, a very fine performance overall), and Bernstein (with the New York Philharmonic on Sony, not the Vienna Philharmonic on DG).

All of this energy attracts an initially hesitant response from the woodwinds in their transition passage, and then they, too, try a more flowing, expanded variation of their previous music before the march breaks in, grander then ever with the last note of each phrase held for rhetorical emphasis. The furtive transition to the next variation shunts the music into a minor key, but the mood isn't sad or particularly dark. Indeed, the wonderful transformation of the theme that Beethoven gives the flute, clarinet, and bassoon has a quizzical, nonchalant quality that's unforgettably charming. As if surprised by its unusual expressive demeanor, the orchestra pulls up short and gets back on track with a loudly triumphant reprise of the same theme, very much in the style of the march, with trumpets and drums.

But this time the march isn't destined to appear; instead, with an upward rush of scales very similar to what you will hear in the introduction to the Seventh Symphony's first movement, the music cuts off suddenly. Woodwinds and then violins instead lead to a magical coda led off by the bassoon, in which bits of the opening tune ride atop a skipping, off-the-beat rhythm in the strings. After one last recollection of the transition between the theme's two parts, the movement decides, not without some hesitation, to end loudly and emphatically with the principal rhythmic figure that has served as the building block of the entire piece.

Before moving on to the scherzo, there are two further points worth considering regarding this andante. The first concerns form. Some commentators (including Donald Francis Tovey, the patron saint of all English-language writers on music) view this movement as a set of variations on two alternating themes, distinguishing between the opening melody on cellos and violas and the ensuing march. Haydn invented this form, unsurprisingly, and Beethoven developed it to its highest level in the great adagio of the Ninth Symphony. This is a perfectly legitimate view and you may well agree with it.

I prefer to regard the two main ideas in this movement as a single unit because they are both based on the same rhythmic figures, are fairly short in duration taken separately, and seem to flow together into a single large paragraph. However, it's worth pointing out the alternative if only to show that questions of musical form often are not written in stone, and indeed comprise part of the subjective experience of listening and may well change depending on the performers' interpretation or your own mood on any given day. The presence of a multiplicity of right answers constitutes part of what gives the music its expressive richness and freshness on repetition.

Second, finding the optimal tempo for this movement is tricky. The best performances usually fall somewhere between eight and ten minutes. I personally prefer versions on the quicker side, such as Dorati's, but it also depends very much on the speed of the surrounding movements. Thus, Klemperer (EMI) can get away with eleven minutes because of his broad tempos elsewhere. Giulini (DG), on the other hand, is even slower than Klemperer, but strikes me as less persuasive because of his quicker first movement and scherzo, which makes the andante too prominent. Perhaps slowest of all is Ferenc Fricsay with the Berlin Philharmonic on DG at more than thirteen minutes. If you happen to hear it you may be either hypnotically fascinated or simply bored. Toscanini and Günter Wand (both RCA) find a very happy medium at about nine minutes, and also pay welcome attention to Beethoven's bass lines.

THIRD MOVEMENT AND FINALE
(PLAYED WITHOUT PAUSE)

The third movement is technically a scherzo, which literally means "joke," and musically speaking comprises a fast dance movement in triple time, having the basic form ABA. What makes this particular exemplar so special, indeed arguably the most expressively radical and forward-looking music in the whole symphony, is the fact that not only does the music reveal not a shred of danceability, it's actually alternately creepy and menacing. Tovey calls it a "dream of terror." Granted, Haydn wrote some dark, even tragic minuets (the scherzo's musical forerunner), but this is the very first in a whole line of spooky scherzos that populate the Romantic repertoire, culminating in the ones in Mahler's Sixth and Seventh Symphonies.

So expressively, the music explores an entirely different side of the symphony's home key of C minor. The main theme, rising out of the depths of the string section, has the same first few notes as the finale of Mozart's 40th Symphony in G minor, a resemblance that Beethoven himself noted in his sketchbook. Truth be told, if he hadn't pointed it out for future generations, no one probably would have noticed, because the actual sound of the music is entirely different. Far more important, and for the most part unacknowledged, is the fact that the first theme is obviously derived from the opening of the Andante. There's a similar rising phrase starting on lower strings, and a similar rhythm to the continuation. This gives the music a "half-remembered" quality that makes it all the more disturbing, an evil transformation of something formerly heard as benign.

The theme that follows this sinister opening also parallels the shape of the andante's principal idea, even down to the transitional woodwind and string exchanges that introduce it, as it's another march, grimly blasted out on the horns, assisted by striding strings. As in the andante, Beethoven has completely obscured any sense that the music is actually in triple time. The feel of the music is clearly "in two." There's a good reason for this. The rhythmic shape of the march reaches back beyond the second movement to the first: it consists of reiterations of the four-note fate motto, originally in 2/4. Here there's no doubt of Beethoven's intentions, and just as we witnessed the first movement's second subject finally giving in to the music's "dark side," so the same thing happens here with the idea that opens the andante.

It's crucial when listening to music of the classical period to always keep in mind that an "idea" may be a tune, or it may be a musical shape, structure, or concept, such as a lyrical melody followed by a march. The idea of "development" in the sonata style is not necessarily limited to clearly defined themes, nor is it restricted to what happens within a single movement. Beethoven is also masterful in his use of the power of suggestion, exploiting a vague but very real resemblance between themes, or even whole paragraphs. Often, and particularly in this symphony, it embraces a larger process that knits the entire work together as a single organism despite its having a wide expressive range articulated in several distinct parts, or movements.

Most scherzos have the form ABA, with "B" being called a "trio." Within this larger framework, each section falls into two repeated halves. In his Fourth Symphony, Beethoven got into the habit of adding a full repeat of both scherzo and trio: ABABA (with sectional repeats). The Sixth and Seventh Symphonies also follow this format, and originally the Fifth did too, but as noted previously Beethoven cut the extra repeat, which was probably a good idea since the scherzo comes back again in the middle of the finale's development section, so we don't really need to hear it so many times.

Beyond these basic generalizations, the "A" section itself has an unusual shape that's naturally suggested by the nature of the melody: a lyrical strain followed by a march. Instead of breaking up the section into two halves, Beethoven sticks to his plan to track the form of the previous movement, and follows the main theme with two variations characterized by different scoring and small alternations in the tunes. The first variation gives the march increasing prominence in the trumpets and timpani, which especially drives home the resemblance to the first movement. In the second variation, Beethoven combines the opening strains with the fate motto as a nagging accompaniment, cutting the march short and bringing the scherzo proper to a surprisingly gentle close with an impressive diminuendo from the full orchestra.

The trio section begins immediately with the most purely rambunctious music in the entire symphony, and a passage that

remains to this day one of the supreme challenges for orchestral cellos and basses. Building in layers up from the bottom,
Beethoven piles on his jolly theme in staggered entries that grow
closer together as the tune rises through the orchestra; this process
is immediately repeated. After a couple of humorous false starts,
again from the cellos and bases, the trio's second half starts out as
an extended variation of the first part, ending almost exactly the
same way. However, the repeat abandons the loud dynamics heard
previously, and executes a brilliantly judged diminuendo in both
volume and texture designed to lead back to the scherzo.

Once again, what purports to be a repeat is not literal, but in
fact another variation, soft and almost sneaky (the third variation,
completing the analogy to the form of the andante right down to
the scoring). It is music on tiptoes, punctuated by the bassoon
used in a way that would become famous almost a century later
in Paul Dukas's *The Sorcerer's Apprentice*. Hesitant woodwinds and
plucked (*pizzicato*) strings slither past, with the march, in particular, transformed into a skeletal remnant of its former intimidating
self. As the music sinks into the darkness of a sustained chord on
the strings, the timpani softly tap out the fate motto, and then the
dotted rhythm of the main themes of the andante and scherzo.
Even this passage of pure atmosphere bears a clear relationship to
what has come before; not a note gets wasted.

Over what has now become a steady throbbing in the drums,
the violins make as if to begin the scherzo all over, but they can't
seem to remember how the tune should go. Their groping for the
correct notes, rising ever higher in an upward spiral, suddenly
ignites the full orchestra and perhaps the most exciting single crescendo in all of instrumental music leads directly, without pause,
into the blazing fanfare for the full brass section that starts the
finale. This moment has a very interesting and equally illustrious
predecessor: the transition from a mysterious C minor to a blazing
C major at the words "And God said 'Let there be light,' and there
was light!" in Haydn's oratorio *The Creation* (1798). Beethoven's
audience would not have missed the resemblance.

Even more significant this likely homage to what was widely considered the most sublime masterpiece in all of music and the definitive statement by the world's greatest living composer marked Beethoven as an artist whose works deal with "big" issues. No other moment in the symphony reveals more tellingly his determination to create music that goes beyond mere entertainment, and to address questions of fate, tragedy, heroism, and even spirituality. This may sound like a lot to read into a single crescendo, but as a symbol of what made Beethoven's purely instrumental music so different from that of his contemporaries and immediate successors, it's a useful perspective to adopt.

This cathartic moment depends for much of its effectiveness on establishing a logical, proportional tempo relationship between the third and fourth movements. Some conductors nevertheless indulge in a tasteless introductory retard before settling down to the quicker main tempo (such as Hermann Scherchen on Westminster, and to a lesser extent Stokowski on Decca), while others give the impression that the music is just slightly out of alignment (like Giulini on DG—just a hair too slow). Furtwängler, in his performance of June 30, 1943, showed that one way to take some extra time over this passage is to hold the crescendo to the point where the listener loses the underlying pulse of the scherzo. This way, a slight prolongation of the first three rising notes of the finale's brass fanfare still conveys the impression of energy unleashed through forward movement. Lorin Maazel, in his superb reading with the Berlin Philharmonic on DG, also manages a similar effect.

That said, and however it's done, the opening of the finale is a moment that seldom fails to make an almost elemental impression in most performances because of the way Beethoven has prepared for its emergence. Most obviously, there is the tremendous release of pent-up harmonic tension that produces such an overwhelming impression of having arrived at a predestined goal. However, beyond the mere mechanics of modulation from one tonal region to another, Beethoven does everything that he can to ensure that we feel the location of this ultimate arrival to be "home," the place toward which the music has been pointing since its very first note.

He accomplishes this larger task using every possible gambit in his compositional arsenal, including having the scherzo lead directly into the finale, and above all in the shape and substance of the themes we now hear. The initial rising fanfare in the brass (with trombones added to the trumpets and horns) obviously recalls the march in the andante, as does the ensuing celebration of dotted rhythms, only here the order of events is reversed (that is, the celebratory fanfare comes first, the passages in dotted rhythm afterwards). It's as if Beethoven is telling us that previously all the elements were in place, but not quite in the optimal sequence to produce the feeling of unalloyed triumph. Now, however, everything is in its proper position.

Beethoven will continue to challenge both our conscious and subconscious powers of memory as this finale proceeds as, after the opening theme with its festively racing strings and dancing rhythms, he continues with the presentation of what turns out to be a sonata-form exposition. These following ideas really do take the form of a pageant or procession. Including the first subject, there are four tunes in all, each introduced (after the opening) by frenzied "motion music" in the strings. Next up is a heroic summons starting with two phrases from horns and oboes (the oboes usually get blown away by the horns, unless the conductor is Otto Klemperer on EMI), followed by a continuation in the strings.

These first two phrases (the ones played by horns and oboes) are answered by chugging chords from the violins and trombones and a wonderfully energetic counter-theme in the cellos and basses that almost never penetrates the texture clearly. You can here it best in recordings by Dorati (Mercury Living Presence), Bernstein (Sony), Szell (Sony), René Leibowitz (Chesky), Toscanini (RCA), Peter Eötvös (BMC), Eugen Jochum (Philips or EMI), Vänskä (BIS), and Klemperer (EMI, noted above). The problem here is admittedly of Beethoven's making, what with the whole orchestra going crazy and a fortissimo timpani roll dominating the bass register, but on recordings at least it's possible to capture just about everything, and this is one of those moments where hearing the lower parts really is important.

The principal job of this tune, beyond continuing the general celebration, is to move away from the home key of C major. It does this from its second phrase on, and you can hear it happen very clearly once you know the symphony well, and can compare how it sounds on this initial appearance with Beethoven's rewrite in the recapitulation to stay in the home key. For now, I just want to point out the difference between the opening theme, which defines the home key, and this one, which goes elsewhere. The initial fanfare and its continuation give a sense of jumping up and down for joy, but remaining in the same place, while this melody soars aloft as if airborne, clearly pointing towards a new destination.

That destination turns out to be the second subject, another of Beethoven's brilliant exploitations of the power of memory. This rollicking melody, initially on the violins, consists entirely of four-note motives very similar to the "fate" motto from the first movement. Even the shape of the tune is broadly similar: a loud statement and soft answer, and then a louder restatement and soft extended answer leading to a climax. The three initial, shorter notes of the main motive are triplets here, while "fate" had straight eighth notes, but the resemblance is unmistakable even though the actual melody is completely different in character. Beethoven has big plans both for this tune and its first-movement cousin in the development section.

As you can see, the two principal subjects of this exposition are constructed entirely from elements that we have heard previously, so Beethoven's big moment of arrival at the ultimate home key of C major is prepared not just harmonically, but motivically and thematically, even though the actual tunes are all entirely new. I can't stress this point strongly enough: if you take anything away from this book, it should be an enhanced ability to recognize ideas as they develop throughout a large work such as this symphony, ideas that go beyond mere repetition of themes to include anything from tiny motives, to larger melodic shapes, to mere instrumental color. This isn't difficult; it's all lying on the musical surface, and if you know where to look and how to listen you will own the key to understanding nearly two centuries of instrumental music in large forms.

The climax of the second subject leads, after more emphatic string gestures, to a cadence theme for the woodwinds in slower tempo (longer notes) designed to round off the exposition in broad and dignified strokes. The full orchestra takes up the tune with increasing energy and a gathering crescendo that leads either on to the development section or back to the beginning if the exposition repeat is observed. Until roughly the 1950s it was the universal custom to omit the repeat, and some conductors do it still. Today, however, most observe all repeats as a matter of course, and when the music itself is so compelling, who can blame them? Nevertheless, it has to be admitted that the lead back to the opening is not one of Beethoven's better transitions. The music itself feels as if it wants to move continuously forward.

This impression is confirmed by the way the end of the exposition spills over naturally into the development section with a loud, long-held chord under which vigorous rhythmic activity in the lower strings once again reminds us that we want to hear Beethoven's bass lines. The second subject immediately intervenes, at first loudly, then in dialogue between the strings and woodwinds. As the volume increases, the trombones announce the bits of the opening fanfare, but you may notice that whereas the finale began with a rising motive of three long notes, Beethoven extends this opening motive to four notes in the development section. This fact offers the best reason for including the finale's exposition repeat, because that extra anticipatory note at the beginning (technically it's called an "upbeat") only gets added the second time around.

As in the first movement, Beethoven then proceeds to deconstruct the fanfare, turning it into a two-note fragment alternating with empathic statements of the second subject's modified fate motive on trumpets and timpani. At last, the fanfare breaks free with what can only be called "hysterical triumph," and piles up into a huge climax that comes to full stop, immediately undermined by a timid decrescendo in the strings. Now comes the crowning stroke of genius that everyone, even Spohr, has always praised to the skies. The march portion of the scherzo returns, softly, almost sheepishly, on clarinets lightly supported by pizzicato strings. This final exorcism of fate represents one of the most brilliant exploitations in all of music of form (practically the same thing as long-term memory) in the service of emotional expression.

Recall that the second subject has served as the main focus of the development section. Now, in recalling the scherzo, not only does its scoring and emotional temperature in context make the music sound completely harmless, but Beethoven presents it as a logical further development of the cheerful second subject. It would be difficult to imagine a more graphic image of fate defanged, subordinated and rendered impotent before this seemingly endless pageant of colossal triumph. As fate slinks by, an apologetic oboe detaches itself and spins out a lyrical line above, yet another suggestion of a prior event: the moving cadenza for the same instrument in the first movement recapitulation. Only now there's no suggestion of pathos, just shyness to the point where it comes as positive relief that a quick crescendo intervenes and ignites the recapitulation.

Now it just so happens that Beethoven had a model for this particular stroke of genius: Haydn's Symphony no. 46 features a finale interrupted by the preceding minuet, and while there is no scholarly consensus that Beethoven was aware of Haydn's similar procedure, what convinces me is that in both cases, what actually returns is the prior movement's *second half*. The resemblance ends there, however, because not only is Beethoven working on a much larger scale, but the emotional ambiance is entirely different. Haydn, quite typically, is playing a joke, one so wacky that the finale never quite recovers and rushes to a finish as if embarrassed with itself. This could hardly be further removed from Beethoven's metaphysical vision, but it's worth pointing out if only to show once again how similar formal innovations can yield hugely different expressive results.

The recapitulation is unusually regular, exactly following the order of the exposition. Its only significant deviation occurs, as suggested previously, in the horn/oboe transition theme which is now modified to steer the music in the direction of the home key, with the result that Beethoven has the opportunity to put the strings' continuation of the theme in the bass (with the usual problems regarding audibility in some performances). After the cadence theme Beethoven cuts directly to the combination of second subject and opening fanfare that led to the reappearance of the scherzo in the development section, only here, after a few sharp chords that threaten to bring the symphony to a premature close, we proceed directly to the famous "coda that just won't quit."

Comedian Danny Kaye used to do a wonderful little sketch featuring this coda, about a conductor who kept turning to the audience to receive applause only to be shocked when the orchestra kept on going. There really is something amusing about this seemingly endless perorating, and why not? Triumph is happy, sometimes even to the point of laughter, but the fact is that Beethoven is trying to solve a problem that turned out to be the bane of composers for at least the next century or more: how to stop effectively. After unleashing such a huge torrent of rhythmic and dynamic energy, he needs to find a satisfying ending that doesn't give the impression of the music running out of gas. Excessive enthusiasm turns out to be just the ticket in this case, but as usual Beethoven's coda does more than just make noise.

You may have noted that Beethoven left two important tunes out of the development section entirely: the horn/oboe transition, and the stately cadence theme. As was the case with the first movement's second subject, he has reserved them for treatment here. The coda starts with a variant of the transition theme on bassoons, then horns, leading to a sweeping passage of descending scales in the violins answered by a rising scale in the solo piccolo. This whole section is then repeated with even more gusto and brighter scoring (note the carefree trill in the piccolo). The tempo then starts to increase, leading to a sped-up version of the cadence theme, and continuing to accelerate into a brilliant final apotheosis of the movement's opening fanfare. Here, after several unsuccessful attempts at suggesting a final chord, the orchestra at last comes to rest on a massive, unison C.

This coda served as the inspiration for countless similar endings during the Romantic period. Brahms's First Symphony and Tchaikovsky's Fourth, to cite only two examples, would have been unthinkable without its example. Dvořák, in his Seventh Symphony, took the idea of "the coda that won't quit" and ingeniously reshaped it to his own ends. Indeed this ending, and the whole idea of tragedy turned to triumph, turned out to be as much a manifesto of the Romantic finale as the mysterious opening of the Ninth Symphony proved an irresistible way to start a symphony (particularly for Bruckner). But the example of the Fifth has also proven dangerous.

Taken as a whole, the Fifth Symphony is bottom heavy. With all of its repeats intact, the finale is (or should be) the largest movement, and the fact that the scherzo is attached only makes the whole complex of continuous music even larger still. Classical sonata form usually reserves the biggest and most complex structure for the first movement, with the remaining parts of a symphony or concerto becoming progressively simpler and lighter. Of course, there are exceptions: Haydn's Symphony no. 98 and Mozart's no. 41 "Jupiter" Symphony might fall into the category of "finale symphonies," but they lack Beethoven's emotional range and heroic demeanor.

Throwing the weight of the symphonic argument—and the requirement to find a convincingly heroic resolution—onto the finale of a large symphonic work turned out to be a tall order, one that few subsequent composers fulfilled with consistent success. When Brahms withheld performance of his First Symphony for nearly twenty years, it was—as he himself admitted—at least partly out of fear of being compared to Beethoven; and we can be sure that if he had specified exactly what about Beethoven he feared most, he would likely have pointed to this finale, so often imitated, but so seldom equaled. The Fifth Symphony remains, to this day, the standard by which music expressing the victory of human striving over the forces of darkness is measured.

Chapter 3

Symphony no. 7 in A Major,
Op. 92 (1812)

1. *Poco sostenuto—Vivace*
2. *Allegretto*
3. *Scherzo: Presto*
4. *Finale: Allegro con brio*

Orchestration: 2 each of flutes, oboes, clarinets, bassoons, horns, and trumpets, plus timpani and strings

THE SEVENTH SYMPHONY made its debut on December 8, 1813, at a charity concert to benefit Austrians and Bavarians wounded at the Battle of Hanau, in which the German forces tried (and failed) to block Napoleon's retreat to Frankfurt after his defeat in the Battle of Leipzig. The German forces suffered some nine thousand casualties over the two days of the battle, which took place on October 30 and 31, 1813. The concert was organized by Johann Nepomuk Mälzel, inventor of the metronome and other musicomechanical devices, including a "mechanical trumpeter" and a contraption called the panharmonicon, for which Beethoven wrote the original version of his "Battle Symphony," *Wellington's Victory*.

Sensing the possibility of an even greater success for Beethoven's patriotic potboiler, Mälzel prevailed upon the composer to arrange the work for a very full orchestra, including lots of brass and the fusillades of rifle shots which have made the piece the natural disc mate on recordings to Tchaikovsky's similarly artillery-laden *1812 Overture*. The best recording of both, by the way, is Dorati's on Mercury Living Presence. Battle pieces have always been popular subjects for musical description, and if you want to add to your library of works commemorating Napoleon's defeats, you can also include Swedish composer Franz Berwald's *The Battle of Leipzig*, composed in 1828.

This being a charity concert for a very specific purpose, the program was very different from the extravaganza of new music heard at the premiere of the Fifth Symphony. It consisted only of the Seventh to lead off, two marches (by Dussek and Pleyel, respectively) for orchestra and Mälzel's mechanical trumpeter, and finally *Wellington's Victory*. The event was a huge success, as much for patriotic as for musical reasons, so much so that the concert was repeated a few days later. There is no denying, however, that the symphony made a very favorable impression, particularly its second movement, which was encored at both concerts. Many of the most famous, or soon to be famous, musicians in Vienna took part, including Moscheles, Hummel, Meyerbeer, and Spohr, whose account, in his autobiography, of Beethoven's conducting has become famous in its own right:

> Beethoven had gotten used to giving expressive indications to the orchestra through all kinds of unusual bodily gestures. Whenever a sforzando occurred, he threw his arms wide with great force, having previously kept them crossed over his chest. In soft passages he would stoop lower and lower until he felt he had achieved the correct level of quiet. If a crescendo followed, he would gradually stand up and at the arrival of the forte jump

into the air. Sometimes he also unknowingly shouted to encourage the orchestra to play louder.

By this time Beethoven was very deaf, and could hear only the loudest outbursts. He conducted as much by seeing what the players were doing as from hearing the results of his gesticulations, and Spohr recounts that he embarrassed himself in rehearsal at one point by getting lost in his own work. He made a terribly sad, tragicomic spectacle of himself, but at the same time confirmed his genius and cemented his reputation as the greatest living composer in the German tradition. For beyond the external forces acting on the creation and initial presentation of the Seventh Symphony, there are purely musical considerations that assume even greater importance, and tell us much more about the character of the music itself.

In order to understand where the Seventh Symphony stands in terms of Beethoven's inner development, it's necessary to return to March 27, 1808, several months prior to the unfortunate premieres of the Fifth and Sixth Symphonies. This was the date of the gala performance of Haydn's oratorio *The Creation* in honor of the aging composer's seventy-sixth birthday. It was also the scene of Beethoven's very public reconciliation with his teacher. Beethoven stood among the crowd of aristocrats who greeted Haydn as he arrived at the hall, and he helped to carry the frail composer in his armchair to his place in the auditorium. A bit over a year later, on May 31, 1809, Haydn died in Vienna, which had by that time been occupied by Napoleon's army.

Beethoven's relationship with Haydn, as already noted in the first chapter, was extremely complex and characterized by both jealousy and paranoia. Although a huge admirer (and sometime imitator) of Mozart, Beethoven's own musical inclinations stood much closer to Haydn's, and yet the pupil's early works hardly withstood comparison to those of the Europe's greatest living composer. Beethoven's Mass in C, composed for the same patron who commissioned Haydn's last six Masses, had been a signal failure, and his oratorio *Christ on the Mount of Olives* paled beside Haydn's *The*

Creation and its companion work, *The Seasons*. Even the massive Third Symphony, the *Eroica*, was more notorious than popular.

Beethoven was much more successful as a composer of chamber music, and his genius was certainly recognized by a growing number of music lovers. But from his perspective, Haydn's remarkable youthfulness and productivity in old age represented a barrier to Beethoven's recognition that Mozart, inimitably great but conveniently dead, never did. All this had changed by 1808—Haydn's output had ceased in 1803; there had been no new symphonies from "the father of the symphony" since the mid-1790s. Beethoven's star was rising, and with it his self-confidence. The Fifth and Sixth Symphonies, composed as a pair, appear in this context as his answer to Haydn's two oratorios, one representing the spiritual triumph of light over darkness, the other a passionate hymn to God in nature.

The spiritual content of the Fifth and Sixth Symphonies led to two new conceptions of the medium: the "finale symphony," in which the weight of symphonic argument is redistributed toward the end of the work, and the "program symphony," in which the music refers to more than just abstract feelings and includes concrete elements that can be legitimately described in sound, such as birdsong, or a storm. In the Seventh and Eighth Symphonies, however, also composed as a complementary pair, Beethoven returns to a more classical conception as developed by Haydn and Mozart. The two works can thus be seen as a tribute to some of the primary qualities of Haydn's symphonies: humor, boundless vitality, and (especially in the Seventh) structural ingenuity.

If the range of expression in these two works is naturally smaller than in their predecessors, the feelings that they do encompass are just as intense, and the compression and rapidity of Beethoven's thought even more pronounced. It's no mistake that the Seventh and the Eighth contain no real slow movements. Haydn's pursuit of what we might call "symphonic spirituality" in his adagios finds no analogue in any Beethoven symphony until the slow movement of the Ninth. In the Seventh and Eighth, though, Beethoven is

content to rediscover and reinterpret the pc
phonic music as a form of grand entertainmen*
the desire to evoke anything external or progr
add depth or significance.

ORCHESTRATION AND SOUND WORLD

The scoring of the Seventh Symphony precisely matches that established by Haydn in his last six symphonies, and used by Beethoven in his First and Second. There are no additional instruments such as piccolo or trombones, as in the Fifth and Sixth, or the extra horn that we find in the Third. But if you believe these relatively slender forces yield a small sound, think again. The orchestra makes a huge impact, as befits this very large symphony (the Seventh is in fact about five minutes longer than the Fifth in most performances, adjusted for repeats). No orchestral work of Beethoven's has a more thrilling sonority than this symphony, because much more important than how many instruments play is how they actually are used.

The Seventh's orchestration has a new openness to the sound, evident in the wide spacing and rich timbre of the very first forte chord for the full ensemble. Beethoven uses his woodwind section with extraordinary freedom throughout the work, not just as a block in opposition to the strings (as we often find in the Fifth), but with a keen sense of the individual color of each of its constituent members. The main theme of the first movement seems to embody the very soul of the flute; the frosty chord for oboes, clarinets, bassoons, and horns that opens and closes the allegretto makes an unforgettably bleak impression; the scherzo further exploits the timbre of the flute in every possible combination, first with bassoons, then clarinets, then oboes.

Indeed, it's probably fair to say that distinctiveness in orchestration stems largely from a composer's handling of the woodwinds, because it is this section that has the largest variety of timbres within its family. This means there are an unlimited number of ending combinations as well as rewarding solo possibilities, and nowhere does Beethoven exploit this potential as vividly as in this symphony. The wind instruments are treated less as flashes of color added to the basic string ensemble, and more as equal partners throughout. This is especially evident in the trio of the scherzo, where the long sustained notes for the violins become, at the forte reprise, loud solo blasts on the trumpet requiring great breath control and stamina.

The symphony's special sonic character becomes even more evident in considering Beethoven's treatment of the horns, and here he is not so much exploiting a new sound as rediscovering an old one. It's probably fair to say that no timbre in the orchestra conveys more steely tension than horns played in their high register, particularly when their sound comes from within a tutti. The sound of the horn seems to light up the entire orchestral passage. Haydn was the first major composer to exploit this texture in his early symphonies in C major. Consider especially the famous "Maria Theresia" Symphony no. 48. He had no choice; the orchestra at his disposal had no trumpets, and so he was forced to use horns instead. Later in his career, and particularly in his 88th and 90th Symphonies, this type of scoring became a noteworthy personal feature of his style.

Until the Seventh Symphony, Beethoven's model of basic orchestral sonority had been Mozart, who was able to use his wind section to achieve a remarkable warmth and sensuality of color. He did this by freeing up his bassoons from the general bass line and by blending timbres in the lower to middle registers. Mozart detested the flute and loved the mellow tone of the clarinets. Haydn's scoring is brighter, edgier, wider in register, and notably leaner in ensemble passages. Those thrilling high horns in the outer movements of Beethoven's Seventh, the numerous important flute solos, and the trumpet blasts in the trio of the scherzo, all stand squarely in the orchestral tradition of Haydn, and give the symphony an impact and sheer physicality unmatched in any other of Beethoven's orchestral works, exciting as they unquestionably are.

LARGE-SCALE FORM

If the Fifth Symphony shifted its weightiest music toward the finale, the Seventh does just the opposite, beginning with one of Beethoven's largest opening movements, or more correctly, pair of movements. Slow introductions to first movement allegros are not new; they were a specialty of Haydn's, and Beethoven adopted them in his First, Second, and Fourth Symphonies as well. But this introduction isn't particularly slow, and it is so huge that it really does have its own independent form. In the Fifth Symphony, Beethoven linked the scherzo to the finale, and in the Sixth "Pastoral," he unites the last three movements: the scherzo, "Storm," and final "Hymn of Thanksgiving." The Seventh continues this practice, but does so in terms of the classical precedents that Beethoven consciously emulates throughout the work.

The "Storm" (fourth) movement in the "Pastoral" Symphony is usually considered both as an independent movement as well as an introduction to the finale. So it is, too, with this introduction, which actually lasts as long or longer than the Sixth's "Storm" in most performances—about four minutes. This is also close to, or exceeding, the length of the scherzos of the first two symphonies, or the allegretto scherzando second movement of the Eighth. In creating a new kind of "slow" first-movement introduction, then, Beethoven establishes a type of polarity, or conflict, right at the beginning of the symphony, that he will explore by stages as the work proceeds.

This purely musical conflict consists of the tension between duple and triple meters, and it plays out like this:

First Movement
Introduction: 4/4 (solemn confidence)
Vivace: 6/8 (carefree happiness)
Second Movement (Allegretto): 4/4 (elegiac nostalgia)
Scherzo (Presto): 3/4 (childlike simplicity)
Finale (Allegro con brio): 2/4 (exhilarating strength and unquenchable optimism)

Note the elegance of what in twentieth-century terms would be called an "arch form," to use Hungarian composer Béla Bartók's term: a symmetrical pattern comprised of alternating duple and triple meters. In fact, the symmetry extends well beyond the time signatures. As you will see, the movements in duple time all share certain basic features, as do those in triple time. Additionally, whereas the first movement keeps these shared elements separate and distinct between its two sections, the finale combines them and thus, like the finale of the Fifth, constitutes a genuinely satisfying culmination of the entire symphony.

So the Seventh Symphony really does tell a story, presenting an initial, basic duality and tracing its progress toward an ultimate resolution, but it does so in purely musical, nonprogrammatic terms. This story is broadly shaped by the tempos and rhythmic structures outlined above, and articulated in detail by the emotional content of each movement—in other words, by the tunes. However, as you will shortly see, what makes the melodic content of the Seventh so special is the unusually close relationship between the main themes and their underlying rhythms. When Wagner somewhat misleadingly called the Seventh Symphony "the apotheosis of the dance," it was this power of expression through the sheer force of rhythm that he had in mind, and it's an idea that will permeate the discussion that follows.

One final word before moving on to explore Seventh Symphony movement by movement: when I talk about Haydn and Mozart as influences on Beethoven, the point is not to minimize his originality, but rather to place him in his musical context. Indeed, it's much easier to hear what makes this music unique when it is compared directly to the pieces that exercised the strongest formative influences on it. Furthermore, Beethoven's significance as a composer rests on his position in the musical continuum that both preceded and succeeded him, and the more familiar you become with some of the other pieces mentioned over the course of these discussions, the more you will get out of Beethoven as well. After all, these were the works that he also knew and admired, by the composers in whose shadow he worked.

In short, you certainly don't have to know Haydn's 88th or 90th symphonies to understand Beethoven's Seventh, but it certainly can't hurt. In fact, one of the best aspects of a musical culture full of all kinds of similarities, homages, and even some blatant and not-so-blatant copying, is that you can listen to the most popular and important works both for their own sake, and also as a guide to further exploration. I would be remiss in discussing Beethoven's symphonies if I did not spend at least some time giving you the tools to take advantage of this rewarding possibility and pursue it at your own convenience.

FIRST MOVEMENT

Introduction

Rhythm in music can be understood on both small and large scales; the former includes the duration of individual notes, or the shape of short, distinct motives (such as the fate motto from the Fifth Symphony). Large-scale rhythm concerns how these basic units build up into longer phrases and sentences—in other words, melodies—over many bars of music. Fundamental to this latter quality are two numbers: four and eight. The overwhelming majority of tunes, whether internally repetitious or totally free-form, break up into rhythmically regular sections of four or eight bars and their multiples (sixteen, thirty-two, etc). When a composer chooses to ignore this balanced arrangement of phrases, the music accordingly sounds unusual, often with exciting or surprising results, because it defies the listener's expectations. Knowing how to vary phrase length artistically thus becomes an extremely important tool in preventing monotony and preserving freshness and vitality.

I'm sure you can see, then, that if a composer chooses to work with melodies that have a very symmetrical structure (that is, that are based on the repetition of simple rhythms in regular two, four, or eight bar increments), supple phrasing matters a great deal. Now it just so happens that all of the duple-meter principal themes in this symphony, in the introduction, second movement, and finale, employ a particularly extreme form of this type of symmetrical melody, one almost certainly modeled on Haydn's Symphony no. 88. In that work, the first movement allegro, minuet, and finale all use tunes which consist, at least initially, of four short phrases, the first three of which are identical in rhythm, and the last one, which starts the same way but evolves into a cadence—a brief pause, or slightly expanded close, that rounds off the melodic period.

To hear how this works most clearly, jump ahead to the second movement's opening theme: three repetitions of the same five-note rhythm, followed by an abbreviated repetition with the last note chopped off. The resulting silence has exactly the same function as a comma does in a sentence: it allows a short pause for breath before the music continues, and because you expect to hear the fifth note that never actually comes, you listen through the pause and understand intuitively that even though there is no sound for that one moment, the phrase has not actually finished.

Alternately, Beethoven may also choose to make the fourth repetition of the basic rhythmic unit longer, expanding it into a phrase of somewhat different character. This is what you hear in the initial eight bars of the first-movement introduction. If this still isn't clear after listening a few times, consider the popular show tune "America" from Leonard Bernstein's *West Side Story*. The refrain, from its beginning at "I like to be in America," through the words "for a small fee in America!" consists of four phrases in identical rhythm, exactly as you find in Haydn's 88th and Beethoven's Seventh. This comparison emphasizes the closeness of both composers to the world of popular song, and to their unashamed delight in creating catchy tunes with genuine mass appeal.

Beethoven seems particularly adept at writing difficult openings. You would think a simple chord for full orchestra would be easy to play together, but evidently it isn't. Many performances, some of the them excellent, "spread" the chord, an effect you can hear because the timpani stroke that underpins it usually comes in either just ahead of, or slightly behind, the rest of the orchestra.

Of course, Beethoven intends this; he wants a big, resonant sonority, and the violins, which for this purpose have to play a four-note chord, *must* arpeggiate—that is, play the notes rapidly in sequence from the bottom up. So a certain amount of spread to the tone is inevitable. Still, this initial sound still should be a sharp stroke, and not the kind of "boom-chick" smear that you hear, say, in a famous broadcast recording from the mid-1930s featuring Wilhelm Mengelberg and the Concertgebouw Orchestra of Amsterdam (on Tahra).

As I mentioned previously, this "slow introduction" is not in fact all that slow. Beethoven marks it *poco sostenuto*, or "a little bit sustained," which hardly gives a firm indication of its tempo. In any case, it should not be played like a dirge. The music has to flow, and more to the point, relate logically to the ensuing *vivace* main section of the movement.

Beethoven's opening melody is as basic a representation of the number four as you could possibly imagine: four loud chords for full orchestra, each followed by a four-note, bell-like motive in even half notes lasting two bars (the loud chord includes the first note), played in turn by solo oboe, two clarinets, two horns, and finally second oboe, two bassoons, and soft strings. Atop this chiming bit of melody the woodwinds spin out an increasingly elaborate lyrical counterpoint. This disguises some of the rhythmic regularity of the opening and eventually turns it into a nine-bar phrase.

The irregularity continues as violins and violas softly intone three rising scales, separated by gentle comments from the clarinets and bassoons. These exchanges make up a complex of five bars, an odd number both literally and figuratively. The last set of scales enlists the woodwinds and horns in a big crescendo, leading back to a fortissimo restatement of the opening bars, accompanied all the while by lively scales moving from the bottom of the basses to the top of the violins. This bottom-to-top process is one of the qualities that gives the music its uniquely expansive sonority, the feeling of the orchestra playing at the full extent of its range in terms of both dynamics and pitch. Beethoven will exploit this fundamental idea many, many times in the music that follows, just as he will also use simple scales as a unifying idea that recurs in every movement.

I mentioned that this introduction is so long as to have its own independent form. Here it is: AABAB, and you have just heard the first two "A" sections. "B" consists of a hesitant, gentle strain for oboes, clarinets, and bassoons in broken rhythms, quietly oscillating between just a few notes, softly accompanied by a brief motive in the violins starting with a trill. This lasts six bars, followed by a five-bar lead-back in crescendo to the loud version of "A." Pay particular attention to this passage, both the woodwinds and the trilling violins; it's going to have the most astonishing consequences later on. As it stands, the unusual phrase length sets up a basic tension between the two main ideas of the introduction. The return of "A," in particular, comes more as an interruption than as a smooth succession. The dissonant harmonies lend a more insistent, urgent quality to it than previously.

So far we have heard "A" three times, each time more emphatically. "B" remains a calm voice whose steady crescendo is always cut short. This musical round-robin could go on forever, and seems to have every intention of doing so, except that just when you expect "A" again Beethoven sharply interrupts its impending return. The woodwinds, perhaps assuming that they now have the field to themselves, return to the mood (but not the melody) of "B," and are rebuffed twice, at first loudly, and then by the suggestion of something new based on the even sixteenth-note rhythms of the scale figures that have figured so prominently. The flute starts playing the note E, echoed by the strings. Tossing Es back and forth (a total of sixty-one times, says Sir George Grove), the rhythm becomes "dotted," tripping along in a new meter (6/8) to the repeated "dum dadum dum dadum" that has since become famous, and we find ourselves in the main body of the movement.

Vivace

All the talk of phrase length in the preceding section might lead you to believe that you are supposed to be conscious of this aspect of the music, but you aren't. So don't even think of counting measures! You should hear "flow." The whole point of music that consists of dramatic action in real time is to avoid anything that constricts or prevents freedom of movement. Variations in phrase length counteract the tendency toward stiffness produced by the symmetrical structure of the melodies themselves. Also, note that Beethoven has not specifically asked for an accelerando leading to the Vivace. He has composed it into the transition. When the main theme arrives, it is thus already in the new tempo, and this above all else tells us that the *poco sostenuto* introduction need not be that slow, nor the Vivace unusually quick. "Vivacious" is as much an indication of general character as it is of relative speed.

It says everything about the special sound of the Seventh that its instantly catchy and memorable main theme is the first in any Beethoven symphony that is not played by the strings. As I noted previously, its scoring represents "the soul of the flute," but in fact this is just the predominating instrument. At various points the flute is joined by the clarinets and bassoons, and then the oboes, creating between them a kind of "superflute" tone than has extra strength and color as well as characteristic brightness of timbre.

The melody itself, up to the first forte entrance of the strings, actually has the traditional sixteen bars falling into two eight-bar halves. But its second half is interesting in that it achieves its length by including two interruptions by the strings echoing the woodwinds, and these seem to stretch the melody beyond its natural length. So when Beethoven immediately repeats the theme fortissimo (technically called a "counterstatement"), giving the tune to those gloriously ringing high horns and violins, leaving out the two echoes, and accompanied by the omnipresent galloping dotted rhythm, the resulting compressed version has an extra physical power and energy.

The structure of the rest of the movement comprises Beethoven's most telling homage to Haydn. It is in monothematic sonata form of the type pioneered by the older composer, in this case openly modeled on the first movement of Symphony no. 88. "Monothematic sonata form" is something of a misnomer, since it suggests that the entire movement contains only one theme, which is usually not the case. What it really means is that the music continuously generates new themes from the material of the exposition's first subject. In other words, it is continually evolving, making the distinction between "exposition" and "development" academic.

Remember that the purpose of the "exposition" is not so much to present tunes, but to establish key areas and to convey the feeling of motion away from the home, or "tonic," key. Although Beethoven reserves his Haydnesque "4 x 4" melody for the introduction, both the Seventh Symphony and Haydn's 88th feature first-movement expositions based on repeated rhythmic figures that drive the music forward to the point where the second subject need only be a tiny reflection of the first. But this doesn't mean that there is any dearth of melodic material—just the opposite.

Even the choice of meter, 6/8, is a distinctly Haydnesque feature. Because of its ability to alternate freely between duple and triple time and its lightness at quick tempos, 6/8 is usually reserved for finales rather than more weighty symphonic first movements. Indeed, one reason why Beethoven precedes the vivace, and its main theme in particular, with a long introduction is because the principal subject would be inconceivable all by itself as the beginning of a big symphony. This was precisely Haydn's tactic in two of his latest and greatest works, Symphony no. 101 ("The Clock") and Symphony no. 103 ("Drumroll"), both of which have impressive introductions to first movements in 6/8 time.

After the fortissimo version of Beethoven's main theme has run its course, the orchestra continues charging forward, generating one tune after another from the basic galloping rhythm. This makes it possible for Beethoven to use what are in fact two new, completely fresh melodies, but still have them sound clearly related to everything else. And this is the real beauty of monothematic sonata form. If you want to hear the actual second subject, listen for a series of eight loud two-note jabs from the strings and woodwinds, followed by a sudden diminuendo. The woodwinds then enter with a sweet little four-bar phrase in the usual dotted rhythm answered loudly by the strings. Technically, these four bars comprise the essence of the second subject. This is followed by a long crescendo in the strings assisted by a chirping oboe, leading to a double climax and the eventual return of the main theme in imitation between the upper and (often hard to hear) lower strings, which rounds off the exposition.

So, as you can hear for yourself, the music hasn't been so much "monothematic" as "monorhythmic," and unlike the corresponding passage in the Fifth Symphony, with its two big, separate paragraphs each containing two sentences, this whole exposition comes across as a single, sweeping statement containing several different tunes, all joined together by their shared rhythm. The overall impression is of continual forward progress driving a process of perpetual melodic evolution.

Another of the great advantages of monothematic sonata form, at least from Haydn's point of view, is that it is "front-loaded"—it allows the maximum amount of variety and eventfulness to be packed into the smallest possible space. Where Beethoven differs from his teacher is in applying this same technique on a much larger scale. Haydn's monothematic sonata-form movements, such as the one that opens Symphony no. 88, are exciting because of their compactness. This one has all of the older composer's excitement and variety, married to a wholly new expansiveness and grandeur. The result, in a word, is colossal in every sense.

British conductor Thomas Beecham, who was no fan of Beethoven's later symphonies, and who was as famous for his one-liners as for his exuberant performing style, quipped that the scherzo of this symphony reminded him of "a lot of yaks jumping about." Beecham's EMI recording of the Seventh, whatever reservations he might have had aside, remains one of the best. He really lets the horns rip in the first movement and finale, and he joins Herbert Blomstedt (Berlin Classics/Brilliant Classics), George Szell (Sony Classical) and Nikolaus Harnoncourt (Warner Classics) among those who exploit Beethoven's sonic concept particularly well. One of the worst in this regard, by the way, is Herbert von Karajan on DG (particularly his 1977 Berlin recording), who drowns his winds in a welter of strings and timpani. If you want to hear the Berlin Philharmonic at its finest in this music, try Joseph Keilberth's version (also on Warner).

The reason I bring up Beecham here is because his jumping yaks are very much in keeping with the music at the end of the exposition, and the image returns not just in the scherzo, but in the finale too. You can't miss this wonderfully funny, cartoonlike moment as the strings and off-the-beat winds and timpani hiccup their way through a rising scale and then suddenly stop dead in their tracks. At this point Beethoven asks that the exposition be repeated, and frankly this is probably the weakest moment in the entire symphony. On the one hand, it's wonderful to hear the music again and you might argue that the start of the development section (more jumping yaks) is even funnier as a result; on the other hand, the feeling of irresistible forward progress is effectively shattered by going back to the beginning.

For that reason, this is one of the few exposition repeats in Beethoven that you may still hear omitted in concert performance (much less so on recordings), even today when such things tend to be respected as a matter of course. The length of the movement, at twelve to thirteen minutes on average without the repeat, may also be a factor in the conductor's decision, as it would never be in considering the first movement of the Fifth Symphony, where the repeat really is essential. In fact, most of the noteworthy performances listed above (Beecham, Blomstedt, Szell, and Keilberth) ignore the repeat in the first movement, and you really don't miss it—or at least I don't, even though I enjoy hearing it in those great recordings that include it (Bernstein on DG, and Harnoncourt and

Günter Wand on RCA). It really is a question of personal taste rather than musical necessity.

After Beecham's yaks, the development section proceeds in two big waves, and barely a bar goes by in which the dotted galloping rhythm is not present somewhere in the orchestra. First, the strings make a brief allusion to the beginning of the first subject, entering in sequence from the bottom up. This rises to a climax featuring the rhythm alone, without any melody at all, before coming to a sudden halt. The next wave is a mirror image of the first. The woodwinds enter in dialogue from the top down: flutes and oboes, then clarinets and bassoons, with the strings softly jogging along below. Once again a big crescendo leads to an even more vigorous assertion of the movement's primal rhythm, now in a stormy minor key with trumpets and timpani adding to the impact. There's no diminuendo here, only increasingly energetic exchanges between strings and winds plowing inexorably forward to the recapitulation, which sales in on fortissimo violins.

This development section is relatively short, but it is quite remarkable nonetheless. What, in fact, does it develop? The main theme is barely present, and large tracts of it consist basically of crisscrossing scales with no discernable melody at all. Beethoven's main concern is to highlight the raw power of the basic dotted rhythm at all dynamic levels, and through all the sections of the orchestra. Because all of the vivace's thematic material is based on this same rhythm, the concept of "development" is fulfilled by the simple fact that everything will naturally sound related to everything else, leaving Beethoven free to explore the most effective possible means of transition back to the first subject. So the lack of melodic interest, far from being a disadvantage, makes the moment of arrival at the recapitulation even more powerful as a result.

This development section also solves a very interesting problem in musical aesthetics. This concerns the conflict between highly distinctive melodies and the goal of sonata form—tonally directed development. It's a problem that challenged (and defeated) many composers in the later, more "tune-oriented" Romantic period.

British composer and conductor Constant Lambert said it best when he pointed out, concerning composers who liked to use actual folk music in their larger works, that "the only thing you can do with a folk song is play it louder."

In other words, the very notion of "development" destroys the only thing worth quoting: the distinctive melody in its entirety. The main theme of Beethoven's Seventh is not a folk tune, but its catchiness and melodic originality make it the next best thing. It is surely significant, then, that Beethoven only alludes to it over the course the development section, understanding that trying to "do something" with it would be much less satisfying than making its return—in all of its pristine glory—one of the most gratifying moments in the whole work. Hence a short, almost athematic development section is just the ticket in this particular case, and the handling of form arises directly from the nature of the movement's thematic material.

When it returns, and as we already heard happen in the development section's two phases, the first subject is presented as the mirror image of its original self:

EXPOSITION (FIRST SUBJECT):

Statement (piano)	Counterstatement (fortissimo)
Theme: Woodwinds (string "echoes")	Strings/Horns
Accompaniment: Strings	Full Orchestra

RECAPITULATION (FIRST SUBJECT):

Statement (fortissimo)	Counterstatement (piano)
Theme: Strings (woodwind "echoes")	Woodwinds
Accompaniment: Winds and Timpani	Violins

As you can see from the chart above, the whole order of presentation is inverted. What was formerly soft is now loud, and what was given to the woodwinds now goes to the strings, and vice versa. It's a breathtaking combination of imaginative freedom while maintaining the formal symmetry that characterizes so much of the music of the Classical period, and which Beethoven never forgot no matter how wild his music became.

There are other differences, too. The onset of the recapitulation features a wonderful galloping bass line not present originally, one of so many moments that need to penetrate the texture more clearly on recordings than they usually do (the recordings already named are all very good in this regard). Also, the counterstatement on the woodwinds, led by the oboe, veers off in the tune's second half toward a reflective minor key, and this is as close as Beethoven ever gets to actually varying his main tune in the manner often found in a typical development section. The transitional music to the second subject is slightly abbreviated so as to get there more quickly, but the section ends as before, with Beecham's jumping yaks.

The coda begins with yet another yak joke: one of the yaks gets left behind and gives an embarrassed little hop rather than a healthy leap. As in the first movement of the Fifth Symphony, the coda continues the business of the development section, only since Beethoven largely ignored his first subject there, and since the second subject has no independent existence, he ignores it here as well. Accordingly, the thematic material is new but still based on the omnipresent dotted rhythm.

First, there's a wonderful slow crescendo for violins and sustained woodwinds over a grinding, repeated bass line. Be sure to listen through the texture to that persistent tugging at the bottom of the orchestra. Beethoven will do this again in the first-movement coda of the Ninth Symphony. At the height of the crescendo, the full orchestra breaks in with another new theme in the dotted rhythm, and with a few more robust exchanges between string and winds the movement blazes to a close, with pealing horns well to the fore.

Haydn's Symphony no. 88, by the way, also has a coda featuring a double climax giving special prominence to the horns.
But the Seventh Symphony had just as large an influence on later
composers. Some works you might want to check out with the
sound (and in particular the rhythm) of the Seventh's first movement in mind are:

Berlioz: *Harold in Italy* (third movement, "Serenade")

Dvořák: Symphony no. 5 (trio of the scherzo)

Tchaikovsky: Symphony no. 4 (first movement)

Mahler: Symphony no. 7 (first movement)

Martinu: Symphony no. 5 (finale)

Guaraldi: *It's the Easter Beagle, Charlie Brown* (cartoon soundtrack)

Whatever debt Beethoven owed to the past he repaid
amply, not just in terms of his own reinterpretation of those
earlier influences, but also in the rich legacy he bequeathed to
the many composers who found themselves inspired by what he
achieved here.

SECOND MOVEMENT

In Beethoven's day this allegretto turned out to be a "greatest hit"
in every sense of the word. It was encored in the symphony's first
performances, and even occasionally substituted for the much
lighter second movement of the Eighth Symphony to give that
work additional weight and seriousness. As a welcome emotional
counterbalance to the almost giddy happiness characterizing the
rest of the Seventh Symphony, it's absolutely perfect in its place,
but the music also displays a level of beauty and polish that makes
it one of Beethoven's supreme utterances in any medium. For
many listeners, it remains the finest part of the symphony, and in
this respect Beethoven again pays homage to Haydn, who often
reserved his most outstanding strokes of genius for his slow movements (think of Symphonies no. 44 "Mourning," 94 "Surprise,"

100 "Military," and 101 "Clock," all named after their famous slow movements).

"Slow" in this context is of course a relative term, as this allegretto should not be played at a dirgelike tempo despite the main theme's stylized funeral march character. Most performances last somewhere between seven and a half and nine minutes. A little bit less works very well (Mackerras on EMI), as can a bit more (Günter Wand on RCA), but anything over ten minutes (Stokowski on Decca; Furtwängler on EMI) really is pushing the music beyond where it clearly wants to go. Even Sergiu Celibidache, the mad genius of slow tempos (Munich Philharmonic on EMI), doesn't exceed ten minutes in an otherwise deathly dull performance. Roger Norrington, at just over six and a half minutes in his latest cycle for Hänssler Classics, probably constitutes the limit at the opposite tempo extreme. Szell (Sony) to my mind is ideal.

Beethoven chose his tempo carefully to emphasize the critical role that rhythm plays in the Haydnesque "4 x 4" main theme. In fact, the tune contains exactly sixteen bars (twenty-four if we consider the fact that the second half is usually repeated), with the first eight featuring only three different pitches across the three and four-fifths repetitions of its five-note basic rhythm. The second half uses more tones and thus is more melodic, but the rhythmic scheme is absolutely identical. Only a flowing tempo gives the rhythm the insistent quality that Beethoven's extremely careful phrase markings suggest it should have. A lot of musicological ink has been spilled over the correct way to stress the simultaneously dotted and tied last two notes of the basic motto, with the options ranging from Harnoncourt on the one hand (short staccato on the last note) to Bernstein on the other (more sustained treatment).

The formal scheme is quite simple: ABAB—coda (A), but within these sections Beethoven offers an astonishing wealth of detail and a great deal of development. There's practically no literal repetition, despite the simplicity of that opening theme. The movement can be classed either as the kind of sonata-without-development-section structure favored by Mozart, in which the recapitulation is actually a varied restatement of the exposition, or it can be categorized as a close relative of Haydn's typical variations on two themes, one minor, the other major. The truth is that this seemingly rudimentary structure contains a little bit of everything, inventing itself as it proceeds with an improvisatory freedom that goes a long way towards explaining the music's endless fascination and popularity. Let's look more closely.

After a marvelously gaunt decrescendo chord for all the wood-winds (minus flutes) plus horns, Beethoven builds up his initial "A" section as a miniature set of variations:

Theme: Violas, divided cellos, and basses. The divided cellos give an extra richness to the orchestra's lower end throughout this part of the movement, while the shifting harmonies put musical flesh on the theme's bald rhythmic outline. The repetition of the theme's second half is marked down to pianissimo from the initial piano.

Variation 1: The theme, now in the second violins, becomes an accompaniment to a gorgeously sad countermelody given to the violas and top half of the cellos. It fits onto the theme like an ornate vine growing on a trellis. For convenience's sake, I will call this new melody the "descant," and its appearance reflects a tendency to use counterpoint (combining multiple melodic voices) that will bear spectacular fruit later on in the movement.

Variation 2: First violins have the theme, second violins get the descant, and the remaining strings accompany with a rich harmonic filling. As you can now hear, the only thing that Beethoven varies is the scoring and dynamics of this combination of themes, rather like an early prototype of Ravel's *Boléro*, or the "evil forces" march in the first movement of Shostakovich's Seventh "Leningrad" Symphony. The theme's relative brevity, its haunting intertwining with the descant, and the noble sadness of the harmony all prevent any suggestion of monotony from creeping in. The repeat of the theme's second half initiates a crescendo and the first entrance of the woodwinds (oboes and bassoons), leading to:

Variation 3: Horns and woodwinds have the theme, fortissimo, punctuated by trumpets and timpani. The first violins play the descant. Now the second-half repeat makes a decrescendo, and the final bar of both theme and descant, played one extra time, serves as a transition to the "B" section. Note the rhythm of this last bar of the theme used as a transition: long–short–short–long.

The contrasting theme appears as the antithesis of what we have just heard. Over a rippling, triplet accompaniment in the violins, the woodwinds sing out a sweetly nostalgic, lyrical melody in constantly changing tone colors: clarinets and bassoons, then with flutes and oboes added. Beethoven is very close to Mozart in his handling of the wind section here, nowhere more so than in his use of soft trumpets instead of horns for extra harmonic support at the end of the first phrase (a feature that Mozart exploited brilliantly in his opera *Cosi fan tutte*).

The lyrical tune dissolves into a dialogue between clarinet and horn in descending and ascending scales; then the whole wind section rhapsodizes over suspenseful harmonies in a manner that would later exert a big influence on Brahms in his slow movements. The dialogue returns, and with an abrupt crescendo the descending scale charges through the entire string section only to be brought up short with a series of rough two-note tugs from strings, then brass and timpani, and then the woodwinds.

Beyond the astonishing richness of luscious woodwind timbre that characterizes this whole section, it's also worth mentioning that Beethoven takes great pains to make his phrases overlap and vary considerably in length. Remember that the first part of the movement consists of a rhythmically rigid theme articulated in absolutely regular eight-bar phrases. This new idea features phrases of all different lengths. There's no need to go into the technicalities; what you hear is simply a perpetually flowing melody. Suffice it to say that when the dialogue in scales returns for the second time, in flute, oboe, and bassoon, it ends the section with a phrase of eleven bars, and this is what makes the sudden descent and those abrupt two-note tugs so jolting. They really do cut the music off at the knees.

The return to the "A" section is, to put it mildly, highly varied. Flute, oboe, and bassoon have the descant, and this unvarying tone color in contrast to what preceded it gives the melody a decidedly monochrome, mournful quality. The original rhythmic theme accompanies softly in pizzicato second violins, cellos and basses, but you may not notice it embedded in the rapid accompaniment in running sixteenth notes divided between the first violins and violas. Toward the last phrase of the descant, trumpets and timpani enter softly, injecting a note of menace into an already grim picture.

The running sixteenth notes continue into the next section, an extensive fugue based on the beginning of the theme's second phrase. Contrapuntal writing like this always tempts composers on account of its being perceived as learned and serious, but there's always a risk that it will sound somewhat foreign in its otherwise nonpolyphonic surroundings. Such is arguably the case with the fugal writing in the finale of the "Eroica" Symphony. It was a problem that Beethoven wrestled with throughout his career, but he has prepared for this episode beautifully by accustoming us to counterpoint in the guise of the main theme and its descant melody.

This example, then, stands as one of the most natural and emotionally apt examples in his entire output. Beethoven allows himself sufficient time to work out a subdued, whispered conversation between the various string sections. The fugue subject enters in the following order: first violins, second violins, cellos and basses, and lastly violas, making for four independent voices in all. Oboes and bassoon join in as if to add a fifth voice, but a swift crescendo from the strings ushers in a repeat of the main theme for all the strings, brass, and timpani, with the entire woodwind section keeping up the accompaniment of running sixteenth notes.

The same transition as before, for oboes, clarinets, bassoons, and horns, leads to an abbreviated return of the "B" section, which doesn't get any further than its first phrase before the main theme returns on flutes, clarinets, and bassoons and initiates the coda. Alternately loud and soft statements in the rhythm of the theme's last bar clearly suggest that the orchestra is seeking an ending, but Beethoven has one last surprise in store. The theme returns yet again, differently scored for each repetition of its basic rhythm: flutes and oboe, oboe and clarinets, bassoons and horns, then pizzicato strings—a sequence repeated for the theme's second half as well. Oboes, clarinets, bassoons, and horns repeat the last bar once again, long–short–short–long, followed by pizzicato strings which, at last taking up their bows, utter a loud sigh that fades into the same chord that opened the movement.

I want to conclude discussion of this movement with two interesting textual notes. Some conductors, most famously Erich Kleiber and his son Carlos (in the latter's DG recording and his much better Philips video) keep the strings pizzicato until the end. This strikes me as less convincing than the bowed version, if only because it renders Beethoven's diminuendo on the first violin's last phrase all but impossible.

You might also have noticed that the opening chord, the final chord, and the transitional passages for woodwind between the movement's "A" and "B" sections are all scored for the identical combination of oboes, clarinets, bassoons, and horns. This is one of those bits of orchestral finesse that always characterizes the work of great composers. You may not be conscious of it in performance, but this emphasis on a kind of "timbral refrain" serves to characterize and unify the music at the primal level of pure sound, and certainly contributes an additional expressive dimension.

THIRD MOVEMENT

This rollicking scherzo offers Beethoven's most clever take on his extended version of the form. You may recall from our discussion of the Fifth Symphony that by this period he liked making the scherzo and trio come around twice, that is ABABA instead of the usual ABA form typical of most previous symphonic minuets and scherzos. In order to get the most enjoyment from the games that Beethoven plays here, though, it's necessary to go into the question of repeats in some detail, and it may surprise you to learn that until recently very few performances actually played this movement as Beethoven intended. Indeed, although the period performance movement has done a lot to legitimize this scherzo's original architecture, you are still likely to encounter abridged versions both in concert and on recordings. Whether this is a good or bad thing remains a question of personal taste, but it's still very nice to know just what Beethoven actually wrote.

Normally, each section in a scherzo (the scherzo proper and the trio) has two halves, both of which get repeated, at least the first time through. Until very recently, most conductors played the reprise of the scherzo without repeats, and there is good historical precedent for this practice, some of which can be found in this very piece. So a traditional scherzo will look like this, showing all of the repeats:

SCHERZO	TRIO	SCHERZO
AABB	CCDD	AB or AABB

And here is Beethoven's scheme for the scherzo of the Seventh Symphony:

SCHERZO	TRIO	SCHERZO	TRIO	SCHERZO
AABB	CCDD	AAB	CCDD	AB

As you can see, the main body of the scherzo loses a repeat each time it returns. In addition, the first time that the scherzo comes back, Beethoven asks that the repeat of "A" be played "always piano" right through to the end of the "B" section. This makes it necessary to observe the repeat scheme there as written;

otherwise it's open season everywhere else, particularly as regards treatment of the trio, which is supposed to be played both times with all repeats intact. Conductors who play the whole movement as outlined above include Harnoncourt and Wand. The very worst offenders in the repeat department are Karajan (DG, his final cycle) and Stokowski. The former strips out all of the repeats entirely, which is defensible, but the latter really goes too far in actually cutting the piece down to a traditional ABA (at a droopy tempo too), making a complete mess of Beethoven's obvious intentions.

What Beethoven obviously intended, and what we so seldom get to hear, is a movement that wants to go round and round chasing its own tail forever, but which actually becomes progressively shorter as it proceeds, thus theoretically preventing monotony. It needs to be played as its *presto* tempo indicates: very swiftly and above all lightly, and it requires great virtuosity and concentration from the orchestra. By the same token the *assai meno presto* (much less fast) trio sections should not be played too slowly. Not only does a dragging tempo sound boring, but the music, which is comical enough as it stands, has a tendency to degenerate into a series of lazy belches and oinks that hardly benefit from being prolonged.

This being a stylized dance movement, the music shares with the first movement vivace a triple-time signature (3/4 as opposed to 6/8) and a monothematic sonata form for its main section. In other words, the exposition is "A," while the development and recapitulation are contained in "B." Naturally this is somewhat rudimentary compared with what we heard in the first movement, particularly as the "A" section is only twenty-four bars long, lasting slightly more than ten seconds. Still, the outlines of the form are quite clear.

Moreover, the thematic material consists almost entirely of three conjoined elements all plainly originating in the first movement:

1. First, as Thomas Beecham pointed out, there are those jumping yaks.
2. Next come scales akin to those that led off the first movement's development section (and popped up yet again in the second movement's lyrical central episode).

3. Finally, and most remarkably, the end of each half of the scherzo's main section is a very literal but much faster quotation of the softly trilling string motive from the first movement's introduction.

Beethoven fuses all three of these elements into a single, capricious theme. The yaks appear primarily at the beginning of both main sections, and also between sections as transitional material. The continuation consists largely of scale patterns, mostly descending, initially in flutes and bassoons, but skipping about from one section of the orchestra to another before the music settles down into the motive with the trills. This really is a piece in which, as we saw in the first movement, Beethoven creates something wonderful out of very few basic elements.

Also like the opening vivace, the development section lacks a clear thematic profile, but for an entirely different reason, arising from the slender nature of the movement's primary material. It's a deliciously comic episode consisting of a tiny five-note motive (first heard toward the end of the first part) that keeps getting hung up on its last two notes, repeating them over and over in diminuendo, interrupted by isolated yak jumps. At last the original theme in scales appears in the solo oboe and leads to the recapitulation, fortissimo, which is a varied, more rambunctious restatement of the first part. That's really all there is to it: good, clean fun and unflagging rhythmic energy made all the more potent by the unpredictable phrasing and sudden loud outbursts.

The childlike trio section offers a classic example of what aestheticians might call "the sublime grotesque," and it needs to be played with a certain amount of care if it isn't to sound simply grotesque and lose the element of the sublime that Beethoven intends. Some commentators have claimed that the melody is an actual folk tune, but whether it is or isn't really doesn't matter. The point is that it sounds like one, a melody of such trivial primitiveness (at least in its first half) that you might wonder what it's doing in a symphony. That Beethoven is perfectly serious is indicated by the number of times he wants it to be repeated, and particularly by the fact that he writes out a varied repeat of the first part. This theme is initially stated in broken phrases by clarinets, bassoons, and horns against a sustained note in the violins, with the flutes filling in the pauses the second time around.

Care must be taken when playing this tune not to exaggerate the hairpin [◇] dynamics, and to give full value to the final quarter note of each three-note motive. Otherwise, the melody tends to sound a bit like a hiccupping wino belching out a warped version of "How Dry I Am." This problem can be exacerbated in the second half, which features a single low horn making a strange oinking sound that becomes positively flatulent in crescendo as the first section returns, fortissimo, on the full orchestra, supported by sustained blasts from the trumpets and fortissimo timpani rolls. It's worth noting that Beethoven marks the horn *dolce* ("sweet"), so when, say, Leonard Bernstein in his otherwise very exciting Sony Classical recording with the New York Philharmonic leans on the horn part a bit too much, the result is probably a touch more ribald than Beethoven had in mind.

Many conductors leave out the repeat of the trio's second half on its second appearance, and once again this is very much a matter of taste. If the basic tempo is on the slower side, it probably makes sense, but you do sacrifice a bit of the music's relentless naïveté. Charles Mackerras on EMI is wonderful here, finding a tempo for the trio that is a bit swifter than usual but wholly natural too. The very ending of the movement is also a joke; when the trio seems to be coming back for the third time, instead five sharp chords for the full orchestra in the original quick tempo slam the door shut once and for all. Beethoven would use the exact same idea even more famously in the scherzo of the Ninth Symphony, with equally funny results.

Nothing is more subjective in abstract music than humor. It is because Haydn is so funny that his music is so misunderstood. Beethoven's musical funny bone operates more fitfully. Part of his gravity is a function of his innate intensity of expression, and some of it stems from his belief in his mission as an artist and his self-conscious desire to write music that deals with major issues. This scherzo, particularly in its trio, contains some of the wackiest music he ever wrote. Set it next to the fugue in the previous movement, and you may well find it shocking that these two kinds of music appear side by side in the same work.

Certainly Beethoven's critics were not amused. An anonymous writer in 1825, quoted in Nicolas Slonimsky's *Lexicon of Musical Invective*, described the symphony as "a composition in which the author has indulged a great deal of disagreeable eccentricity." No doubt he had this scherzo largely in mind. But it is for precisely this reason that, although the Fifth Symphony might be said to strike a more serious note, it's also fair to say that the Seventh offers just as broad a range of expression in its own way. Nowadays its "eccentricities" strike us as entirely characteristic manifestations of genius. Musical depth comes in many forms.

FINALE

The finale of the Seventh is not the symphony's largest movement; indeed, depending on the tempo of the Allegretto and the handling of repeats in the scherzo, it is often the shortest. But like the finale of Haydn's Symphony no. 88, it packs a tremendous amount of density into a very short space. For example, the first movement's expansive vivace was based entirely on its single initial theme. This sonata-form movement, by contrast, not only has two distinct subjects, between them they contain no less than six different ideas. The lavishness of material compensates for the compactness of form, making the music sound big even though it's not a grand finale in the sense that the last movement of the Fifth Symphony is. The other reason that Beethoven loads this movement with so many different themes is that, as a finale, it is no less a summing up of all that has come before than we heard in the Fifth. It simply goes about its business differently.

So before turning to the music, let's take a moment to list in no special order some of the musical elements that we have encountered thus far:

1. Important passages in scales (all three previous movements)
2. Haydn's "4 x 4" melodies in duple time (first movement introduction and Allegretto).
3. Repeated dotted rhythms in triple time (first movement).
4. In the Allegretto, a rhythm of long–short–short–long (the last bar in every phrase of the main theme, the transitions between sections, and the conclusion of the whole movement)
5. Jumping yaks (first and third movements)
6. A coda beginning over a grinding, chromatic bass line (first movement)
7. High horn writing in tutti passages (first movement)

You may well come up with items not on the above list, but it should be proof enough of this finale's effectiveness, not just as a piece of self-contained music in its own right but as the culmination of the entire symphonic journey, to note that every one of the above elements appears there anew.

Finally, from an expressive standpoint the movement's two distinct subjects permit an intermingling of major and minor keys that previously appeared for the most part separately. Until this point, the symphony has offered moods of giddy happiness (first and third movements) and elegiac sadness (allegretto) largely in strict opposition. Now they appear in combination, presented with a ferocious energy that dwarfs anything heard previously, even in this most purely exciting and energetic of all Beethoven symphonies. This makes the final triumphant pages all the more gloriously compelling.

It's a pity that the internal combustion engine hadn't yet been invented in 1812, for if it had I feel sure that the beginning of this symphony would have represented Beethoven's impression of kick starting a motorcycle. These two initial, emphatic jolts may strike you as familiar. Their rhythm, long–short–short–long, or at this tempo "dumdadadum!" is nothing but a sped-up version of the final bar of the allegretto's main theme. It appears either by itself, or leading off almost every bar of the first subject's two main ideas. The first of these is a surging "4 x 4" tune nearly identical in structure to that of the allegretto: two eight-bar phrases, in this case both repeated. The second main idea features four repetitions of the basic rhythm answered by vigorous descending scales first by woodwinds and high horns, next by the violins and violas. This all flies by at high speed, but hopefully not so fast as to blur good rhythm, articulation, and Beethoven's textural layering (as happens under Herbert von Karajan, Gustavo Dudamel, and Mikhail Pletnev, all on DG).

These two themes are remarkable in that they contain very little that could be called a conventional melody. Indeed, so unusual are they that even late into the nineteenth century conductor Felix Weingartner in his book on Beethoven's symphonies felt it necessary to call attention to their unique character. The music seems to consist mainly of elemental rhythm and harmony, and little else. In other words, it operates like large stretches of the first movement's development section, those moments when the Beethoven focused on pounding out his 6/8 rhythm and little else.

Melody returns, however, with the transition theme on the violins that immediately follows. This is yet another "4 x 4" tune in four large phrases quite similar to the horn and oboe melody in the same place and having the same purpose in the finale of the Fifth Symphony. In both cases you can clearly hear the change in harmonic direction in the theme's second phrase as we approach the key of the second subject.

This begins with a violent, minor key shaking for full orchestra in dotted rhythm, an entire stampede of yaks. The violins continue the dotted rhythms quietly with indeterminate harmony, punctuated by sharp jabs from the rest of the orchestra. In fact, this theme is every bit as fixated on its dotted rhythm as was the vivace of the first movement, but note the way that Beethoven compresses the range of incident in his finale. Previously, he offered an ample "4 x 4" introduction followed by the main body of the entire movement in dotted rhythm. Here that contrast is reduced to the two brief subjects of a sonata-form exposition.

Twice the harmony solidifies into something that sounds suspiciously like the four-note bell motive returning all the way from the symphony's introduction, but before this impression sinks in deeply all hell breaks loose in the form of a wild orchestral storm whipped up by vicious runs within its texture from the second violins and violas. In terms of melody, to the extent this passage has any, it is a violent variation of the previously heard jumping yaks, but, even more amazingly, both of these ideas derive from the introduction's "B" theme—that gentle woodwind strain hesitantly making a crescendo by oscillating up and down on just a few notes (hence the reason I suggested that you pay particular attention to this passage in its original place).

Taken as a whole, this exposition constitutes an amazing redefinition of just about every element that this symphony has contained. When you first hear it, you might well feel that all of the material is completely unrelated to what has come before because it is all new, but the better you know the music, the more evident the connections will become. The most important point to keep in mind, as I've said previously, is that musical ideas come in many other shapes and sizes besides mere tunes. Not only is the Seventh Symphony unusually rich in this respect, but its nonmelodic ideas are particularly easy to grasp because most of them are based, as we have seen, on a distinctive treatment of rhythm.

However, this exposition, and indeed this entire movement, also contain several elements that are wholly unique. Perhaps the most obvious of them is that the timbre of the woodwind section is conspicuous by its absence. Despite its many distinct ideas, the entire passage blows by as one vast, dynamic, orchestral tutti. The violins lead throughout, that one blast from the high horns notwithstanding, simply because they are the most numerous and powerful single group of instruments in Beethoven's orchestra (the brass can play louder, but don't have all the notes).

Soft passages appear only in the second subject, and then only briefly. Everything, including melody, harmony, dynamics, and even texture is subordinated to an all-powerful rhythmic drive. Moments such as the exposition's concluding "storm" border on unbridled hysteria and represent an energy so vast that it's constantly threatening to spill over into chaos. In short, one of the most vividly new and unexpected qualities that this music offers is a genuine feeling of danger.

However, as always in this most classical of Classical symphonies, even the wildest passages operate within the bounds of a basic formal symmetry. The movement's craziest single moment, the "storm," actually leads back to the beginning of the exposition, and it just so happens that this repeat stands as one of Beethoven's best prepared because the entire exposition operates at such a high level of frenzy that there's no discontinuity in starting over again. Although it is frequently omitted in both live performance and recordings, I personally really like this repeat because it gives the finale added length, which means a touch more weight and stature when set against the other movements, and it also very nicely sets up the development section, which starts just like the exposition.

Speaking of which, this development also has new and unexpected features. Beethoven's two previous examples, in the first movement and the scherzo, were largely athematic, focusing on rhythm and texture. Here, of course, he has done just that throughout the exposition already, so the development does precisely the opposite. It is based almost entirely on the opening theme. At first the lower strings question where it seems to be going, but eventually it settles down to a full repetition, complete with repeats of both halves, in a new harmonic position. This dissolves into a free episode consisting of sequences constructed out of a two-note fragment, tossed back and forth between strings and woodwinds. At last, in what seems like the only woodwind solo in the entire movement, and one of the movement's very few passages of genuine quiet, the orchestra calms down and gives the opening theme to the solo flute.

This moment of tranquility turns out to be short-lived. Its sole purpose is to prepare for the sudden crescendo that leads straight back to the recapitulation. However, because the first theme dominated the development section, Beethoven presents only its first half (with repeat) here, cutting immediately to the second idea with its ringing horns. The transition theme then works its harmonic magic, changing the music's direction and permitting the remainder of the exposition to follow in its original sequence. Beethoven actually intensifies the concluding storm this time around, as if that were possible, and the return to the movement's opening rhythmic jolts seems to suggest the reappearance of the first subject yet again.

But no—the transition theme intervenes and sinks down through the string section. The harmony darkens, and the coda begins over a grinding bass line exactly as in the first movement. Swirling strings and flickers of light from the trumpets and timpani punctuate the cloudy harmony produced by sustained woodwind chords. Like a sunbeam breaking through dark clouds, the vista rapidly brightens and in a flash the orchestra returns to the first subject's second theme, with its brilliant descending scales for high horns and violins. In a last recollection of the symphony's introduction, the violin scales now take over the texture completely, at first descending, and then at the climax reversing direction and rising into the stratosphere. Beethoven lets us hear this process twice, but gives the last word to the transition theme, pealed out by horns and followed by just a hint of the previous storm, now completely devoid of menace and wholly celebratory. A final flurry of scales capped by two sledgehammer rhythmic jolts brings the symphony to its jubilantly frenzied close.

Why, you may ask, does Beethoven use his transition theme to round off this movement? We can't ever really know, but aside from how wonderful it sounds in its own right, consider the following possibilities: it is the most purely melodic idea in the entire finale, and at the end of the day Beethoven always celebrates human feeling in the form of vocal melody. It is also the only idea in the entire movement not clearly derived from something that we have heard earlier. It is entirely typical of Beethoven that, having taken such pains to stress the interrelationships between the themes of the finale and the other movements in the symphony, he would end by emphasizing the music's uniqueness and individuality. It's a notion that could very well stand for the entire work—indeed, for Beethoven's whole life and career.

Recommended Recordings

THERE ARE LITERALLY hundreds of recordings of the Fifth and Seventh Symphonies, many of which are extremely good. The standard of performance in this music has always been high, and there are versions for every taste. Broadly speaking, Beethoven interpretation falls into two categories, the "traditional Germanic" and the "modern Toscanini." Like all such generalizations, this one has limited applicability, and many performances share elements of both approaches because they aren't in any meaningful way mutually exclusive.

Toscanini and his followers liked to claim strict adherence to the score, which was in fact seldom actually the case (just consider the handling of repeats). On the other hand, the traditional German approach of sensible tempos, relentless monumentality, and a dark, weighty sonority accounts for some of, say, Klemperer's gravitas, but hardly his lack of sentimentality and woodwind-prone bias (despite slow tempos), or Furtwängler's spontaneity and fire, for that matter. Furthermore, the historical performance practice movement has added a whole new category, or categories, of possibilities, because not only are there interpretations based on the stylistics of Beethoven's own day, but also attempts at re-creating different stages of the music's subsequent history through the late Romantic period.

In the end it all comes down to personal choice, and what I have tried to do in listing, in no particular order, ten superb performances of each symphony, is to present a broad range of interpretive options in recordings that best embody them. Not all of these recordings may be available at the same time, but most can be located through various online sources, either as mail-order CDs or good-quality digital downloads. Furthermore, even performances that I criticize in the body of the text may have special qualities that make them worth hearing (Giulini's and Fricsay's DG recordings of Beethoven's Fifth, for example).

So, the list below is by no means exhaustive, but it is representative, and I can assure you that all of the performances are excellent examples of their type, and well worth your time and attention. And if you don't already have strong preferences for particular artists, orchestras, or interpretive approaches, you will undoubtedly find yourself developing them very quickly. I list conductor, orchestra, and label, in that order, alongside any other information that may be helpful in locating the right recording. Jump in, and happy listening!

SYMPHONY NO. 5

WILHELM FURTWÄNGLER, Berlin Philharmonic Orchestra, Tahra (Live performance of June 30, 1943)

Furtwängler is back in vogue and enjoys a large cult following among both music lovers and professionals. In the 1940s he foolishly allowed himself to be used by the Nazi regime as the icon of German musical supremacy, and this legacy continues to taint his reputation (and deservedly so, in my opinion). Always an inspirational artist, when he was "on" he was sensational. Unfortunately, much of the time he wasn't, and when you add to this his dislike of studio recording conditions, the result is a legacy that consists largely of unauthorized broadcast performances with terrible sound, full of mistakes that no conductor of his standing would have sanctioned for general release. Happily, this very grand recording of the Fifth ranks with the finest performances he ever gave, and was well recorded for its era, too.

LORIN MAAZEL, Berlin Philharmonic Orchestra, DG [Australian Eloquence]

Despite having recorded a complete Beethoven cycle in Cleveland for Sony Classical (then Columbia), Maazel has never been known for his work with this composer. Early in his career, when he was music director of the Berlin Radio Symphony Orchestra, he recorded the Fifth and Sixth with West Berlin's "other" orchestra, the Philharmonic, and the results, in the Fifth especially, are spectacular. Precision, youthful fire, and the orchestra's natural affinity for the work all combine to provide one of the most satisfying versions ever recorded. It all culminates in a finale that will blast you out of your seat. This little-known but inexpensive and readily available performance (thanks to Australia's "Eloquence" Universal Classics sublabel) deserves a home in every serious Beethoven collection.

ANTAL DORATI, London Symphony Orchestra, Mercury Living Presence

Antal Dorati had a curious career. Known as a generalist, with a particularly affinity for colorful twentieth century scores, he was in fact a terrific Beethoven conductor, as this Fifth clearly shows. Razor sharp rhythms, pellucidly clear textures, and swift tempos offer plenty of excitement, while his second movement is arguably the best paced of all of the quicker versions. His complete cycle with the Royal Philharmonic has long been unavailable (it never made it to CD), but you should at least hear this performance, as well as his Sixth (coupled to this Fifth) and Seventh (with an equally brilliant selection of Beethoven overtures).

OTTO KLEMPERER, Philharmonia Orchestra, EMI, or Vienna Philharmonic Orchestra, DG and Testament
(Live performance of May 25, 1968)

Klemperer has a reputation as the mid-twentieth century's ultimate German conductor, one who favored slow tempos and massive grandeur above all other qualities. In this regard he out-Furtwänglers

Furtwängler (who was not in fact noted for slow tempos). But Klemperer was in fact a modernist earlier in his carrier, a big fan of Stravinsky and a pioneer of sorts in the authentic performance of Bach. So don't let the slow tempos of some of his allegros fool you—it is the dry-eyed grit and determination of his later performances that makes them so powerful. His studio recordings of the Fifth for EMI (one in mono, and a later one in stereo) are fully representative of him, but his live performance from Vienna has a genuine sense of occasion that's quite special.

GEORGE SZELL, Cleveland Orchestra, Sony Classical, or Vienna Philharmonic Orchestra, Orfeo
(Live performance of August 24, 1969)

If Klemperer can be said to out-Furtwängler Furtwängler, Szell out-Toscaninied Toscanini, turning in performances of staggering discipline and ensemble virtuosity, particularly those made with his own Cleveland Orchestra. He was always at his best in Beethoven's Fifth (and Seventh; see below). He made two commercial recordings in stereo, this one and one for Philips with the Concertgebouw Orchestra of Amsterdam, but his live performance from the 1969 Salzburg Festival is in a class of its own, one of the greatest live recordings of anything that has come down to us. Szell was a tough guy, and the often rhythmically casual Vienna Phil plays for him as if their lives depended on it. Even better, you get equally wonderful versions of the Third Piano Concerto (with Emil Gilels, no less) and the *Egmont* Overture—in short, the entire concert, on a single disc. It doesn't get any better.

CARLOS KLEIBER, Vienna Philharmonic, DG

This famous performance has served as the studio recording of reference for several decades, and deservedly so. It's stunningly played, perfectly paced, and as fiery as anyone could ask. As with Szell's live recording with this orchestra, Kleiber clearly has the Vienna Philharmonic working overtime, and you might argue that to get results such as this in a studio environment constitutes an even greater achievement. I personally prefer Szell for the total package, but you can't go wrong here, and this recording is easy to find and reasonably priced. The Seventh that comes with it, however, is not as fine (if you want Kleiber's Seventh, go with the Philips video, even if you will have to watch the sweat dripping off of his nose).

OSMO VÄNSKÄ, Minnesota Orchestra, BIS [SACD]

Stunningly recorded in both regular stereo and multichannel surround formats, Finnish conductor Osmo Vänskä has a real feel for Beethoven's special brand of eruptive energy. Both he and his excellent orchestra seem aware of the history and responsibility that undertaking a new Beethoven cycle entails, and they rise to the occasion impressively. Vänska's performance is a bit like Kleiber's in its combination of excitement and discipline, but he also takes into account some of the ideas of the period performance movement and uses the latest critical edition of the scores. The mean sonority of the Minnesota Orchestra is a touch lighter, too, in keeping with the approach. This doesn't make the performance less weighty; indeed, Beethoven's bass lines come through even more clearly than they do in Vienna. Coupled with an equally fine Fourth Symphony, this disc stands as one of two recent complete symphony cycles that will set the standard in this music for the twenty-first century.

PETER EÖTVÖS, Ensemble Modern, BMC

Here's a real "sleeper" of a performance if ever there was one. Avant-garde composer Peter Eötvös and the chamber group Ensemble Modern decided to approach the Fifth as a radical piece of contemporary music, compensating for the small size of the performing forces using spot microphones as necessary. The result, to be honest, isn't all that different in sound from what Antal Dorati achieves with no such help, but the performance really is fresh and exciting, and certainly not "radical" in the sense that it disfigures the score. Quite the contrary: the playing is staggeringly fine, and the interpretation unfailingly sympathetic. Of course, it comes coupled with some pretty frightening music by Eötvös himself, but as a telling example of Beethoven's timeless relevance this is an awfully impressive release.

RENÉ LEIBOWITZ, Royal Philharmonic Orchestra, Chesky

Leibowitz was a disciple of Schoenberg and a devotee of the latter's atonal dodecaphonic (serial, twelve tone) school of composition. He was also one of the first conductors, in the early 1960s, to take Beethoven's metronome markings seriously. Granted, his colleague Hermann Scherchen beat him to the punch in his 1950s Westminster cycle, but then Scherchen was something of a kook on the podium (fun as that could be). It was Leibowitz's very impressive credentials as a hard-core serialist and academic that made him a force to be reckoned with. Consider that this fast, edgy, and occasionally rough-and-ready performance was captured at exactly the same time as Klemperer's and you will have some idea of just how radical Leibowitz's approach must have seemed in its day. It has, in fact, held up very well, as have the sonics, making this version genuinely prophetic as well as enjoyable in its own right.

IGOR MARKEVITCH, Lamoureux Orchestra, DG

Igor Markevitch is another conductor who, like Antal Dorati, is best known for his dazzling recordings of twentieth-century music, especially Stravinsky, but also for his exceptionally fine complete Tchaikovsky symphony cycle on Philips. A very interesting and distinguished composer in his own right, he brings an analytical eye and razor-sharp intellect to this tautly argued performance. That doesn't prevent him, however, from turning in one of the most exciting renditions of the finale around, aided in no small degree by an orchestra whose distinctly French timbre (bright and slightly acidic woodwinds, tangy brass) sets the music ablaze in a visceral way that you seldom hear anymore. Hard to find, but definitely worth a listen if you happen to stumble across it.

SYMPHONY NO. 7

HERBERT BLOMSTEDT, Staatskapelle Dresden, Berlin Classics
or Brilliant Classics

Blomstedt's complete Beethoven cycle with what is arguably
Germany's greatest orchestra (less known in the West than it
should be, owing to its years behind the Iron Curtain) remains one
of the finest, and now it's one of the cheapest, too. If his version of
the Fifth is a touch underpowered, the same cannot be said for this
Seventh. The forward balances of the woodwinds and horns lend
the music a robust, rustic flavor that's unforgettably characterful,
and the conducting in the finale has plenty of the necessary drive.
This is a performance that wears particularly well because it is
so rich in the basic musical values of crisp ensemble, excellent
balances, and transparency of texture.

GÜNTER WAND, NDR Symphony Orchestra, RCA [formerly
Deutsche Harmonia Mundi]

A self-proclaimed "old conductor of the new school," Günter
Wand in the 1990s, at the very end of his life, found himself
acclaimed as the "grand old man" of German music, much as had
Klemperer. Like his predecessor, he played a lot of contemporary
music in his earlier career, but then focused almost exclusively on
the German classics of Beethoven, Brahms, and Bruckner (with
some Schubert, Schuman, and Mozart thrown in), for which he
was justly acclaimed. This Seventh really does seem to marry
Toscanini's rhythmic discipline with traditional German warmth
and solidity. Wand takes all repeats, even in the scherzo, but the
playing is so fine and the interpretation so loving you'll never
notice the extra length.

LEONARD BERNSTEIN, Vienna Philharmonic Orchestra, DG

Bernstein had a special feeling for the Seventh Symphony. It was
the last work he ever conducted in public, with the Boston Symphony, a performance issued on disc and (sadly) one to be avoided.
This version with the Vienna Philharmonic is the best rendition of

the symphony that both conductor and orchestra have left us. As Carlos Kleiber discovered to his disadvantage, this music is not a natural "fit" for the orchestra (unlike the Fifth). It doesn't always sit well with this ensemble's dark-toned, string-heavy Romantic style. Happily, Bernstein's recording has everything: plenty of fire, clean rhythms, a suitable timbral edge, and a genuine sense of occasion. Bernstein insisted on recording his entire Vienna Beethoven cycle live, and it really pays off here. A classic.

GEORGE SZELL, Cleveland Orchestra, Sony Classical

At times Szell can be overly controlled, but when he's at the top of his game, as he is here, he's just about unbeatable. This performance gets all of the tricky parts of the symphony absolutely right: the balances with the horns and the tempo of the scherzo's central trio section, and it features perhaps the most prefect recording of the famous allegretto that you will ever hear. Szell's tempo and above all his phrasing of the main theme build the first section to a climax of positively breathtaking inevitability. It's absolutely miraculous. You may retain a preference for other versions in considering different interpretive details, but if you want to hear what that allegretto ought to be, then Szell's your man. And the rest is terrific, too.

PAAVO JÄRVI, Deutsche Kammerphilharmonie Bremen, RCA [SACD]

Along with Vänska's Minnesota Orchestra Beethoven cycle (cited above in connection with the Fifth Symphony), Järvi's new set of the complete symphonies looks set to become a pace-setter for many years to come. These performances combine the basic approach of the historical performance movement with playing of absolutely transcendent virtuosity on modern instruments. There is simply no finer symphony cycle by a chamber orchestra. The world of classical music is inherently backward-looking, and full of whiny negativism about the lost "golden age" of conductors, singers, pianists, recordings, etc., etc., *ad nauseum*. It's so refreshing, then, to hear today's performers respond to this music with such elemental excitement, higher technical standards than anything in past eras, and a real point of view—further proof that great Beethoven interpretation is alive and well. The sonics are terrific too, whether in regular stereo or SACD surround-sound formats, and the coupled Fourth Symphony is every bit as splendid.

ARTURO TOSCANINI, New York Philharmonic, RCA (1936)

"This was orchestral performance of a kind new to all of us. The clarity of texture, the precision of balance, the virtuosity of every section, every solo-player with the orchestra—then at its peak— in the service of self-effacing integrity . . . set new undreamed-of standards literally overnight." So said George Szell about the impact of Toscanini's New York Philharmonic during its 1930 European tour. This legendary performance has all of those qualities; it represented nothing less than a revolution in what constitutes great Beethoven playing. Quite well recorded for its day, and perfectly listenable still, its luster has hardly dimmed. The very quick tempo of the scherzo's trio still sounds surprising, as does the finale, which does not try to set a speed record, but achieves its overwhelming power cumulatively, through control of rhythm. One of the most historically important recordings ever made.

NIKOLAUS HARNONCOURT, Chamber Orchestra of Europe, Warner Classics [formerly Teldec]

Nikolaus Harnoncourt is widely and correctly regarded as the founding father of the period instrument movement, which is ironic in that his conducting, however historically informed, often turns out to be as eccentric as any wild-eyed Romantic. His mostly excellent Beethoven cycle (only the Sixth disappoints) used modern strings and winds, with "authentic" brass and timpani to give the sound a more cutting edge. This works wonderfully in the Seventh, one of the cycle's highlights, and a performance that offers plenty of characterful touches (I mentioned previously the phrasing of the allegretto's main theme), splendidly enthusiastic playing, and a welcome lack of affectation. Harnoncourt also observes all repeats, and makes you relish every one of them.

THOMAS BEECHAM, Royal Philharmonic Orchestra, EMI

The man who thought the scherzo sounded like a bunch of jumping yaks also brings us a performance of boundless energy and good-natured appeal. Beecham was one of those artists whose infectious *joie-de-vivre* shines through all of his best performances, and this is certainly one of them, a rousing, take-no-prisoners account that moves as if self-propelled. Blessed with a particularly powerful horn section, Beecham lets it bray away to its (and our) heart's content, and the mid-twentieth century stereo sonics have held up extremely well. This performance doesn't get much attention nowadays, which is surprising given the readiness of British critics to stand up for the nationalist cause no matter how dubious, so let this American be the first to say: Britannia Rules!

JOSEPH KEILBERTH, Berlin Philharmonic Orchestra, Warner Classics [formerly Teldec]

Where, might you ask, in the listings of fine performances from Berlin, is the late, great Herbert von Karajan? Well, if you compare any of the performances featuring "his" orchestra (including Cluytens's cycle on EMI), you might well feel as I do: the playing is often stunningly beautiful, and there are some sterling successes with the Ninth and (arguably) the Fifth Symphonies. Still, at the end of the day, and despite often quick tempos, Karajan reveals little feeling for essential aspects of Beethoven's style: his roughness, his rhythmic snap, stabbing accents, and colorful writing for woodwinds. For example, Karajan's three recordings of the Seventh for DG feature dazzlingly swift finales, increasingly neutered by an all-pervasive surface slickness, with balances weighted toward the violins at the expense of all other instruments. The version from the 1963 complete cycle is the best of the lot. Keilberth, on the other hand, noted as a superb Wagner conductor, lets Beethoven be Beethoven, and the orchestra follows him with a will. The scherzo could perhaps be a little peppier, but the other three movements are pretty uniformly fabulous.

CHARLES MACKERRAS, Royal Liverpool Philharmonic Orchestra, EMI

Australian Charles Mackerras, in his quiet way, has probably had a bigger impact on music in the second half of the twentieth century than just about any other conductor. He single-handedly made the operas and orchestral music of Czech composer Leoš Janáček international repertory items and popular favorites. He composed the delicious ballet *Pineapple Poll*, based on the music of Arthur Sullivan. His pioneering work in the field of historical performance practice set the stage for the movement's successes in the 1970s and '80s. Mackerras's catholicity of taste is matched by a naturalness and an unfailing musicality that characterizes everything he does. In this respect he is very much a successor to Thomas Beecham, as this infections, bubbly, horn-happy account of the Seventh attests (it comes coupled with an excellent Fifth Symphony, by the way). I have already mentioned his ideal handling of the scherzo, but Mackerras is also one of the few conductors who, with the coda of the finale already blasting by at full tilt, still manages a real triple-forte where Beethoven demands it. If you can't find this recording, the more recent one for Hyperion, recorded live with the Scottish Chamber Orchestra, is just about as good.

COMPLETE CYCLES

No Beethoven cycle is perfect as regards all of the symphonies, but many show an extremely high level of accomplishment throughout. If you are looking for a complete set of "The Nine," here are seven of the most highly respected (again, in no particular order):

- Szell/Cleveland Orchestra (Sony)
- Bernstein/Vienna Philharmonic (DG)
- Barenboim/Staatskapelle Berlin (Warner Classics/Teldec)
- Wand/NDR Symphony Orchestra (RCA)
- Blomstedt/Staatskapelle Dresden (Brilliant Classics)

Historical

- Toscanini/NBC Symphony (RCA)

Period Performance Practice

- Harnoncourt/Chamber Orchestra of Europe (Warner)